Reflective Teaching:
An Introduction

REFLECTIVE TEACHING
AND THE SOCIAL CONDITIONS OF SCHOOLING
A Series for Prospective and Practicing Teachers
—Daniel P. Liston and Kenneth M. Zeichner, Series Editors—

❖ ❖ ❖

Zeichner/Liston • Reflective Teaching: An Introduction
Liston/Zeichner • Culture and Teaching

Reflective Teaching: An Introduction

Kenneth M. Zeichner
University of Wisconsin, Madison
Daniel P. Liston
University of Colorado at Boulder

LEA LAWRENCE ERLBAUM ASSOCIATES, PUBLISHERS
1996 Mahwah, New Jersey

Copyright © 1996 by Lawrence Erlbaum Associates, Inc.
All rights reserved. No part of this book may be reproduced in any form, by photostat, microfilm, retrieval
system, or any other means, without the prior written
permission of the publisher.

Lawrence Erlbaum Associates, Inc., Publishers
10 Industrial Avenue
Mahwah, New Jersey 07430

Cover design by Gail Silverman
Cover art by Danny Silverman

Library of Congress Cataloging-in-Publication Data

Zeichner, Kenneth M.
Reflective teaching : an introduction / Kenneth M.
Zeichner, Daniel P. Liston.
p. cm.
Includes bibliographical references (p.) and index.
ISBN 0-8058-8050-X (pbk. : alk. paper)
1. Teaching. 2. Education—Social aspects. 3. Critical
pedagogy. I. Liston, Daniel Patrick. II. Title.
LB1025.3.Z45   1996
371.1'02—dc20   96-18074
                                                CIP

Books published by Lawrence Erlbaum Associates are printed
on acid-free paper, and their bindings are chosen for strength
and durability.

Printed in the United States of America
10 9 8 7 6 5 4 3

This book is dedicated to our children:
Aaron, Jordan, and Noah Zeichner
and Matthew and Ira Liston

CONTENTS

4. DEPICTING AND CONNECTING TEACHERS' THEORIES AND PRACTICES: THE STUFF OF REFLECTION 34

5. TRADITIONS OF REFLECTIVE TEACHING 51

6. FURTHER EXPLORING THE TRADITIONS 63

SERIES PREFACE

AN ESSENTIAL SERIES INTRODUCTION

Whereas many readers rarely read introductory material, we hope you will continue. The success of this book depends, in large part, on how you use it. In what follows we outline some of our key assumptions and we suggest ways for approaching the material in each book of this series entitled, "Reflective Teaching and the Social Conditions of Schooling." First we identify some of our reasons for creating this series. We then relate a bit about our dissatisfaction with how teacher education is usually conducted and how it can be changed. Finally we outline suggestions for ways to best utilize the material in this and subsequent texts.

About 4 years ago we were asked to develop further the ideas outlined in our book *Teacher Education and the Social Conditions of Schooling* (Liston & Zeichner, 1991). It was suggested that we take our basic approach to teacher reflection and our ideas about teacher education curricula and put them into practice. The proposal was attractive and the subsequent endeavor proved to be very challenging. It never seems easy to translate educational "shoulds" and possibilities into schooling "cans" and realities. But we think (and we hope) we have made progress in that effort by designing a series of books intended to help prospective, beginning, and experienced teachers to reflect on their profession, their teaching, and their experiences. We are pleased and delighted to have the opportunity to share this work with you. We hope you will find these texts to be engaging and useful.

We are two university teacher educators, both former elementary teachers, who have worked in inner-city, small town, and suburban elementary and middle schools. We are committed to public schools as democratic institutions, as places of learning in which people of all walks of life come to learn how to live together in a democratic society. Although we are personally committed to ways of working and living together that are much more collaborative than exist today—we are educators first, realists second, and dreamers third. It is our firm belief that an education that engages prospective and practicing teachers' head and hearts, their beliefs and passions, needs to be fair and honest. We have not written these texts to convince you to see schools and society as we do but rather to engage you in a consideration of crucial issues that all teacher need to address. Once engaged we hope that you will be better able to articulate your views, responses, and responsibilities to students and parents, and come to better understand aspects of your role as a teacher in a democratic society.

IMPACTS OF THE SOCIAL CONDITIONS OF SCHOOLING

Prospective teachers need to be prepared for the problems and challenges of public schooling. All to often the focus in schools (departments and colleges) of education remains strictly on the processes that occur within the classroom door and inside the school walls. Many teacher education programs tend to emphasize instructional methodology and the psychology of the learner in the university course work and to underscore survival strategies during student teaching. These are certainly important elements in any teacher's preparation and ones that cannot be ignored. But classrooms and schools are not insulated environments. What goes on inside schools is greatly influenced by what occurs outside of schools. The students who attend and the teachers and administrators who work within those walls bring into the school building all sorts of cultural assumptions, social influences, and contextual dynamics. Unless some concerted attention is given to those assumptions, influences, and dynamics, to the reality of school life and to the social conditions of schooling, our future teachers will be ill prepared.

We are living in a time of remarkable change, a time of social and political transformation. In an era that promises to be rife with social controversies and political difficulties, in which public schooling will increasingly come under attack, during which we will see marked changes in this country's cultural demographic make-up, in which there will be great pressure to transform public schools into private-for-profit enterprises, our teaching workforce must be well prepared. Future teachers cannot, on their own, solve the many societal issues confronting the schools, but they should certainly know what those issues are, have a sense of their own beliefs about those issues, and understand the many ways in which those issues will come alive within their school's walls. Poverty and wealth, our culture of consumerism, what seems to be an increasing amount of violent behavior, and the work pressures of modern life affect the children who attend our public schools. Public attitudes about competition and excellence, race and ethnicity, gender roles and homosexuality, and the environment affect students inside and outside of schools. One can be certain that the issues that affect all of our lives outside of school will certainly influence students inside their schools.

EXAMINING THE SOCIAL CONDITIONS
OF SCHOOLING

Probably the best way to begin to examine contextual issues such as these is to be "watchful" early on in one's professional preparation, to experience features of the social conditions of schooling, and then to examine the experience and what we know about the social and cultural context of schooling. We encourage prospective and practicing teachers to do this. But teacher preparation programs often are not organized in a fashion that would encourage the discussion and examination of these sorts of shared experiences. What traditionally are called *social foundations* courses are typically not school-based, but set apart from some of the more realistic, practical, and engaged dilemmas of schooling. In schools of education we frequently teach what the sociology or philosophy of education has to say about schools but we tend to teach it as sociologists or philosophers, not as teachers struggling with crucial and highly controversial issues. Thus, in our work with prospective and practicing teachers we have developed ways to examine contextual issues of schooling and to enable ourselves and students to articulate our ideas, beliefs, theories, and feelings about those issues. The books in this series attempt to utilize some of these insights and to pass along to others the content and the processes we have found useful.

When students and faculty engage in discussions of the social and political conditions of schooling and the effects of these conditions on students and schools, it is likely that the talk will be lively and controversies will emerge. In this arena there are no absolutely "right" or "wrong" answers. There are choices, frequently difficult ones, choices that require considerable discussion, deliberation, and justification. In order for these discussions to occur we need to create classroom settings that are conducive to conversations about difficult and controversial issues. The best format for such discussion is not the debate, the (in)formal argument, or dispassionate and aloof analysis. Instead the most conducive environment is a classroom designed to create dialogue and conversation among participants with differing points of view. There isn't a recipe or formula that will ensure this type of environment but we think the following suggestions are worth considering.

It is important for individuals using these texts to engage in discussions that are sensitive and respectful toward others, and at the same time challenge each other's views. This is not an easy task. It requires each participant to come to the class sessions prepared, to listen attentively to other people's views, and to address one another with a tone and attitude of respect. This means that when disagreements between individuals occur, and they inevitably will occur, each participant should find a way to express that disagreement without diminishing or attacking the other individual. Participants in these professional discussions need to be able to voice their views freely and to be sensitive toward others. Frequently, this is difficult to do. In discussions of controversial issues, ones that strike emotional chords, we are prone to argue in a way that belittles or disregards another person and their point of view. At times, we try to dismiss both the claim and the person. But if the discussions that these books help to initiate are carried on in that demeaning fashion, the potential power of these works will not be realized. A discussion of this paragraph should occur before discussion the substance raised by this particular text. It is our conviction that when a class keeps both substance and pedagogy in the forefront it has a way of engaging individuals in a much more positive manner. From our own past experiences we have found that during the course of a class's use of this material it may be quite helpful to pause and focus on substantive and pedagogical issues in a conscious and forthright manner. Such time is generally well spent.

UNDERSTANDING AND EXAMINING PERSONAL BELIEFS ABOUT TEACHING AND SCHOOLING

It is also our belief that many educational issues engage and affect our heads and our hearts. Teaching is work that entails both thinking and feeling and those who can reflectively think and feel will find their work more rewarding and their efforts more successful. Good teachers find ways to listen and to integrate their passions, beliefs, and judgments. And so we encourage not only the type of group deliberation just outlined, but also an approach to reading that is attentive to an individual's felt sense or what some might call "gut" level reactions. In the books in this series that contain case material and written reactions to that material, along with the public arguments that pertain to the issues raised, we believe it is essential that you attend to your felt reactions, and attempt to sort out what those reactions tell you. At times it seems we can predict our reactions to the readings and discussions of this material while at other times it can invoke reactions and feelings that surprise us. Attending to those issues in a heartfelt manner, one that is honest and forthright, gives us a better sense of ourselves as teachers and our understandings of the world. Not only do students walk into schools with expectations and assumptions formed as a result of life experiences but so do their teachers. Practicing and prospective teachers can benefit from thinking about their expectations and assumptions. Hopefully, our work will facilitate this sort of reflection.

ABOUT THE BOOKS IN THIS SERIES

The first work in this series, *Reflective Teaching: An Introduction*, introduces the notion of teacher reflection and develops it in relation to the social conditions of schooling. Building on this concept, the second work in the series, *Culture and Teaching*, encourages a reflection on and examination of issues connected to teaching in a pluralistic society. Subsequent works will use a similar reflective approach to examine prominent educational issues and to explore further our understanding of teaching. Topics will include gender and teaching; stories, literacy, and teaching; teaching in a language diverse society; and democracy and teaching. The structure of the works will vary depending on our various contributors, the content of the work, and the ways we can conceive of encouraging reflective practice. But each of the works will take as its central concern the reflective examination of our educational practice within larger social contexts and conditions.

SERIES ACKNOWLEDGMENTS

Two individuals have been essential to the conception and execution of this series. Kathleen Keller, our first editor at St. Martin's Press (where the series originated), initially suggested that we further develop the ideas outlined in *Teacher Education and the Social Conditions of Schooling*

(Liston & Zeichner, 1991). Kathleen was very helpful in the initial stages of this effort. Naomi Silverman, our current and beloved editor at Lawrence Erlbaum Associates, has patiently and skillfully prodded us along attending to both the "big picture" and the small details. We are thankful and indebted to both Kathleen and Naomi.

—Kenneth M. Zeichner
—Daniel P. Liston

Reflective Teaching: An Introduction

PREFACE

This first book in the series Reflective Teaching and the Social Conditions of Schooling is concerned with helping you gain a better understanding of what reflective teaching is all about. In this book, we outline the assumptions and beliefs that distinguish the concept of the reflective teacher from the view of the teacher as passive and as a mere technician, a view that teacher education programs and schools have historically promoted. We also provide some understanding of how various conceptions of reflective teaching differ from one another. We begin our series with a focus on reflective teaching because we believe that as teachers, it is through reflection on our teaching that we become more skilled, more capable, and in general better teachers. There are many kinds of good teachers. Good teaching comes in a variety of packages and forms. Although some types of reflection have us focus more on the content that we teach, others tend to highlight either our students and their learning, or the contexts in which we teach. These are not mutually exclusive conceptions of reflective teaching, they differ in degrees and types of emphasis. Despite these different conceptions of reflective teaching, they all share an emphasis on the importance of examining the thoughts and understandings that we bring to our teaching and the efforts in which we are engaged while we are teaching.

The major goal of both this book and of all of the volumes in this series is to help you explore and define your own positions with regard to the topics and issues at hand within the context of the aims of education in a democratic society. In this work, we focus on the topic of reflective teaching and address a number of issues that pertain to it. The book is subdivided into six chapters. In chapter 1, we provide an initial distinction between reflective and technical approaches to teaching and highlight some of the current issues connected to reflective teaching. In chapter 2, we turn to two influential proponents of reflection, John Dewey, the early 20th-century educational thinker, and Donald Schon, a professor at the Massachusetts Institute of Technology, to develop the foundation of our ideas about reflective teaching. In chapter 3, we build on Dewey and Schon's views through elaborating on teachers' practical theories in a framework offered by Gunnar Handal and Per Lauvas, two Norwegian teacher educators. In this chapter, we examine the role of the teacher's experiences, knowledge, and values in reflective teaching. And in chapter 4, we connect teachers' practical theories and teachers' practices in a conception of reflective teaching. Throughout these first four chapters, we pose a number of questions designed to highlight your assumptions and beliefs about teaching.

Following this elaboration of the characteristics of reflective teaching, we describe distinct orientations to, or what we call the traditions of reflective teaching. In chapter 5, we outline what we mean by a tradition and describe in a fairly succinct manner five traditions of reflective teaching. When individuals talk about reflective teaching, they usually highlight somewhat different aspects of teaching, and in doing so, give a particular emphasis and direction to their understanding of teaching. As noted earlier, some individuals emphasize reflection on the content that they teach and the way in which that content is conveyed to students. This we call the *academic tradition* of reflective teaching. Others maintain that our thoughts should highlight the efficient transmission of knowledge and utilize research-based instructional approaches. This we identify as a *social efficiency* emphasis within reflective teaching. Still another tradition of reflection, the *developmentalist strand*, emphasizes reflection about students, their thinking and understandings, their cultural and linguistic backgrounds, their interests, and their readiness for particular tasks. And there are also those whose concerns direct them toward issues of social justice and democracy, and concerns for equality. This we call the *social reconstructionist* approach to reflective teaching. Finally there is, what we have termed, the *generic tradition*. This orientation simply states that thinking about our teaching is important.

In chapter 6, we provide vignettes that illuminate some of the nuances of each approach to reflective teaching and we discuss what we believe are essential elements for any approach to reflective teaching. In this last chapter, we ask you to react to this series of vignettes depicting teachers' reflections about their work so as to help you formulate your own position about the different conceptions of reflective teaching.

We view this text as an important introduction to the concepts that undergird and inform the idea of reflective teaching. It is a way to introduce a very rich and complex understanding of teaching. But if you were to start and stop with this text, we fear that your introduction to reflective teaching and the social conditions of schooling would be rather limited. The subsequent texts (e.g., *Culture and Teaching, Gender and Teaching*, and provisionally *Stories, Literacy, and Teaching, Teaching in a Language Diverse Society*, and *Democracy and Teaching*) push and pull our understanding of teaching through taking a particular topic or set of issues and asking each of us to reflect on those different issues. We hope that this work provides a basis from which you can then explore further the many issues that teachers and students live and face daily in their classrooms and in their schools.

ACKNOWLEDGMENTS

We thank Todd Dinkelman, Nancy Pauly, and Doreen Ross for their helpful comments about earlier drafts of this manuscript. Landon Beyer, Martha Tevis, and Walter Ullrich read and commented on the entire text. As a result of their suggestions the work improved. We would also like to express a special thank you to Naomi Silverman who has been extremely supportive of our work throughout this project and incredibly understanding and patient with us as we were forced by circumstances to extend our initial deadline.

—*Kenneth M. Zeichner*
—*Daniel P. Liston*

1

UNDERSTANDING REFLECTIVE TEACHING

AN INITIAL DISTINCTION: REFLECTIVE TEACHING AND TECHNICAL TEACHING

- What distinguishes reflective teaching from nonreflective teaching?
- Is there such a thing as a nonreflective teacher?
- If you reflect about your teaching will this necessarily make your teaching better?
- Can reflective teaching be bad teaching?

For many, the term *reflective teaching* sounds redundant. It raises the following questions: In order to teach don't you have to think about your teaching? And isn't such thinking the same thing as reflecting on your teaching? These questions get right to the heart of the matter. In what follows, we argue that not all thinking about teaching constitutes reflective teaching. If a teacher never questions the goals and the values that guide his or her work, the context in which he or she teaches, or never examines his or her assumptions, then it is our belief that this individual is not engaged in reflective teaching. This view is based on a distinction between teaching that is reflective and teaching that is technically focused. In order to make the most of this initial distinction, we first describe a teaching situation and then offer two accounts of the teacher's thoughts about her situation. We begin with a description of her situation.

1

A Student Teaching Incident

Rachel, a White prospective teacher in her early 30s, has been student teaching for 8 weeks in a fourth-grade urban classroom that serves an economically and racially diverse population. For the past few weeks, she and her cooperating teacher have been having a problem with six children (five of whom are children of color from low-income families) who cannot seem to remain engaged in academic activity during the daily 40-minute free-choice period. At times, these students sit and do nothing, whereas at other times they get into arguments with each other and other students, disrupting the rest of the class. Rachel's cooperating teacher, Sue, had long felt that for a part of the school day students should have the opportunity to choose their own activities. Although Sue was not really questioning the value of her approach, she was becoming increasingly frustrated with the students and her own inability to address the situation. Both Sue and Rachel wanted to figure out a way to help these children make more productive use of their time. And both were concerned about the "rough" language used by some of these students when they argued with each other. Sue and Rachel left school that Friday with a sense that a "solution" had to be found. Sue asked Rachel to think about the situation over the weekend and to come back on Monday with some thoughts and suggestions. Sue would do the same.

Teacher as Technician

Initially, Rachel tried to figure out how she could deal with the student disruptions and off-task behavior. She focused on devising ways to present those students with more specific consequences for not complying with the teacher's directions. Rachel remembered the Assertive Discipline Program that she had heard about in one of her university methods courses and thought that she would give this program a try to see if it would lead to an improvement in these students' behaviors. She sensed that her students just didn't understand or feel the consequences for their behavior and that something like the assertive discipline approach might create a framework for sanctions and consequences that would be connected to the students' behavior. Although she didn't want to be the "bad guy" in the classroom she felt that if she didn't demand, sanction, and punish inappropriate behavior the entire class would soon be out of control. She felt that if she and Sue were going to be successful they needed to "get tough."

Teacher as Reflective Practitioner

During a discussion of this situation in her weekly Friday afternoon student teaching seminar, Rachel began to see the "problem" somewhat differently. It was odd she thought, that she had never considered the implications of the fact that all but one of the children that she and Sue had defined as disruptive were "minority" students and from poor socioeconomic backgrounds. Their classroom was very mixed both racially and socioeconomically. Although Rachel was still concerned about developing strategies for helping the six students make better use of their free study time and to decrease the amount of arguing among the students, she also began to ask herself questions about the appropriateness of the classroom's structure in relation to the diverse cultural backgrounds of her pupils. She remembered reading an article by Delpit (1986) in which the author said that not all children benefited from a "liberal" child-oriented, progressive approach to reading instruction and that teachers who taught children of color needed to find ways to make a process approach "fit" and work for all students. Rachel wanted to keep the child-oriented focus of the free-time activity, but thought that she needed to provide a bit more structure so as to facilitate these students' choices. Rachel started to design a classroom intervention for her six students that involved closer planning for and monitoring of the students' activities during the independent study time.

Commentary

In the first teacher-as-technician vignette, Rachel locates the problem entirely in the students and their actions and looks for a program or technique to fix the deviant behavior of her six students. Although Rachel is certainly thinking about the classroom, her thoughts operate from a number of fixed assumptions, assumptions that she does not question. She assumes the problem lies "with the students." She doesn't attempt to examine the context of the classroom or how the students' backgrounds might interact with this context. She also does not seriously question the goals or values embedded in her chosen solution. As a result of this examination, Rachel does not alter the structure of the activity for students but only tries to alter student behavior.

In the second case, Rachel begins to examine her own motivations and the context in which the problem occurs. She then designs an intervention for the specific situation at hand, one that does not locate the problem entirely with the students. Rather than sticking with a number of fixed assumptions, Rachel questions the child-centered approach and what this means in her student teaching situation. In this second instance, Rachel restructures the amount of freedom that students are given during free study period and hopes that this restructuring of the activity will lead to improved student learning and behavior.

When Rachel operated within the technician mode, she accepted the problem as given and tried to solve it. When she was thinking in this mode, the students who misbehaved were seen as the problem. But when Rachel approached the setting as a reflective practitioner, she looked for distinct ways to pose the problem and attempted to get a different purchase on the students and the issues involved. She also questioned her own beliefs and orientations. In what follows, we maintain that the technical approach to thinking about teaching is inadequate. It is a very limited and ultimately, we feel, an ineffectual way to solve educational problems. Although there certainly are many distinct ways to approach reflective teaching, in our view, the teacher as technician is not one of them.

ON REFLECTIVE TEACHING

- Has/did your own teacher education program prepare(d) you to be the kind of teacher who questions the educational goals and the classroom and school contexts and who plays an active role in creating and critiquing curriculum and who considers a variety of instructional strategies?
- When you think about a classroom problem, do you try to see it from different "angles"?
- Do you think that teachers should play leadership roles in curriculum development, program development, and school reform or just stick to their work in the classroom?

During the last decade, the slogan of reflective teaching has been embraced by teachers, teacher educators, and educational researchers all over the world. This international movement in teaching and teacher education that has developed under the banner of reflection can be seen as a reaction against the view of teachers as technicians who narrowly construe the nature of the problems confronting them and merely carry out what others, removed from the classroom, want them to do. The move toward seeing teachers as reflective practitioners is also a rejection of top–down forms of educational reform that involve teachers only as conduits for implementing programs and ideas formulated elsewhere. Proponents of reflective teaching maintain that for much too long, "teachers [have been] considered to be consumers of curriculum knowledge, but are not assumed to have the requisite skills to create or critique that knowledge" (Paris, 1993, p.149). Viewing teachers as reflective practitioners assumes that teachers can both pose and solve problems related to their educational practice. Daily, hourly, even minute by minute, teachers attempt to solve problems that arise in the classroom. The way in which they solve those problems is affected by how they pose or "frame" the problem. Reflective teachers think both about how they frame and then how to solve the problem at hand.

On the surface, the reflective practice movement involves a recognition that teachers should be active in formulating the purposes and ends of their work, that they examine their own values and assumptions, and that they need to play leadership roles in curriculum development and school reform. Reflection also signifies a recognition that the generation of new knowledge about teaching is not the exclusive property of colleges, universities, and research and development centers. It is a recognition that teachers have ideas, beliefs, and theories too, that can contribute to the betterment of teaching for all teachers.

But even today, with all of the talk about teacher empowerment through teacher reflection, we still see a general lack of respect for the craft knowledge of teachers in the educational research establishment. This establishment has attempted to define a so-called "knowledge base" for teaching that excludes the voices and insights of teachers themselves. As Lytle and Cochran-Smith (1990) said:

> The voices of teachers, the questions and problems they pose, the frameworks they use to interpret and improve their practice, and the ways they define and understand their work lives are absent from the literature of research on teaching. (p. 83)

This void must be filled with teachers' voices. Lytle and Cochran-Smith argued, and we agree, that because of teachers' direct involvement in the classroom, they bring a perspective to understanding the complexities of teaching that cannot be matched by external researchers, no matter what methods of study they employ. Although the perspectives of external researchers are helpful in offering a view of schools that cannot be provided by those who work in them on a daily basis and therefore take many things for granted, it is time for the educational research community to recognize and take into account, the issues, and the knowledge of teachers and others who work in schools.

In addition to the invisibility of teacher-generated knowledge in what counts as educational research, many staff development and school improvement initiatives still ignore the knowledge and expertise of teachers and rely primarily on top–down models of school reform that try to get teachers to comply with some externally generated and allegedly research-based solution to school problems. The selling of educational solutions and gimmicks, what some have referred to as "snake oil" staff development, is still big business today. Despite all that the educational reform literature has told us about the futility of reform efforts that treat teachers as mere conduits of others' ideas, the business still thrives.

What these models of research and staff development seem to have in common is a bureaucratic view of teaching, one that views the key to educational improvement as being "the correct definition of procedures for teachers to follow rather than the development of teachers' capacities to make complex judgments based on deep understandings of students and subjects" (Darling-Hammond, 1994, p. 5). In contrast to this bureaucratic view, an understanding of the teacher as a reflective practitioner acknowledges the wealth of expertise that resides in the practices of teachers, what Schon (1983) called *knowledge-in-action*. From the perspective of the individual teacher, this means that the process of understanding and improving one's own teaching must start from reflection on one's own experience and that the sort of "wisdom" derived entirely from the experience or research of others is impoverished.

Reflection as a slogan for educational reform also signifies a recognition that the process of learning to teach continues throughout a teacher's entire career, a recognition that no matter how good a teacher education program is, at best, it can only prepare teachers to begin teaching. When embracing the concept of reflective teaching, there is often a commitment by teachers to internalize the disposition and skills to study their teaching and become better at teaching over time, a commitment to take responsibility for their own professional development. This assumption of responsibility is a central feature of the idea of the reflective teacher.

Initially, then, our understanding of reflective teaching emphasizes five key features, features that we develop further throughout this text. A reflective teacher:

- examines, frames, and attempts to solve the dilemmas of classroom practice;
- is aware of and questions the assumptions and values he or she brings to teaching;
- is attentive to the institutional and cultural contexts in which he or she teaches;
- takes part in curriculum development and is involved in school change efforts; and
- takes responsibility for his or her own professional development.

Although we think these are integral features of what it means to be a reflective teacher, not everyone agrees with us nor do all understand the implications of this view.

THE BANDWAGON OF REFLECTIVE TEACHING

Amidst the explosion of interest in the idea of teachers as reflective practitioners, there has been a great deal of confusion about what is meant in particular instances by the use of the term reflective teaching and whether or not the idea of teachers as reflective practitioners should be supported. Although those who have embraced the slogan of reflective teaching appear to share certain goals about the active role of teachers in school reform and in determining the nature of their own work in the classroom, in reality one cannot tell very much about an approach to teaching from an expressed commitment to the idea of teachers as reflective practitioners alone. Underlying the apparent similarity among those who have embraced the concept of reflective teaching are vast differences in perspectives about teaching, learning, schooling, and the social order. In fact, it has come to the point now where the whole range of beliefs about these issues has become incorporated into the discourse about reflective teaching. Many teacher educators, no matter what their educational orientation, have jumped on the bandwagon at this point, and have committed their energies to furthering some version of reflective teaching practice. According to Calderhead (1989):

> Reflective teaching has been justified on grounds ranging from moral responsibility to technical effectiveness, and reflection has been incorporated into teacher education courses as divergent as those employing a behavioral skills approach, in which reflection is viewed as a means to the achievement of certain prescribed practices, to those committed to a critical science approach in which reflection is seen as a means toward emancipation and professional autonomy. (p. 43)

We are not interested in encouraging you to jump on any bandwagon. Although we believe the reflective teaching movement is a powerful and valuable one, it is not without its problems. One of the central problems has to do with the vagueness and ambiguity of the term, and with a misunderstanding of what is entailed in reflective teaching. Is any thinking about teaching that teachers do reflective teaching? Is any action a teacher takes supportable, just because they have thought about it in some systematic way? We would answer no to both of these questions and will enunciate our fears about the dangers posed by the reflective teaching movement throughout this book. Having initially drawn some distinctions between the teacher as reflective practitioner and the teacher as technician and having identified five key features of reflective teaching, we now elaborate further on what we believe is entailed in a useful and powerful approach to reflective teaching.

2

HISTORICAL ROOTS OF REFLECTIVE TEACHING

We begin our exploration of reflective teaching with a look at some of John Dewey's (1904/1965, 1933, 1938) contributions to promote thoughtful action by teachers. As an early 20th-century educational philosopher, Dewey made many major contributions to educational thinking. He was one of the first educational theorists in the United States to view teachers as reflective practitioners, as professionals who could play very active roles in curriculum development and educational reform. Building on the work of Dewey, we next consider the work of Donald Schon (1983, 1987) and his understanding of reflective practice. Schon has written widely about reflective practice highlighting its uses in several fields such as architecture and medicine. After having examined both Dewey's and Schon's contributions, we then move on to a consideration of recent work in the literature on reflective teaching. Our purpose is not to provide an exhaustive review of conceptions of reflection, but rather to offer a pointed and defensible view of reflective teaching that is distinguished from other views.

DEWEY'S CONTRIBUTION: WHAT IS REFLECTIVE TEACHING?

According to Dewey, the process of reflection for teachers begins when they experience a difficulty, troublesome event, or experience that cannot be immediately resolved, what Hugh Munby and Tom Russell (1990) refer to as *puzzles of practice*. Prompted by a sense of uncertainty or unease, teachers step back to analyze their experiences. As we see, this stepping back can occur either in the midst of the action or after the action is completed.

Much of what Dewey had to say to teachers about the concept of reflective teaching is found in one of his books, *How We Think* (Dewey, 1933). In this book, Dewey makes an important distinction between action that is routine and action that is reflective. According to Dewey, routine action is guided primarily by impulse, tradition, and authority. In every school there exists one or more taken for granted definitions of reality or a "collective code" in which problems, goals, and the means for their accomplishment become defined in particular ways (e.g., "This is the way we do things at our school"). As long as things proceed along without any major disruption, this reality is perceived as unproblematic and serves as a barrier to recognizing and experimenting with alternative viewpoints.

Teachers who are unreflective about their teaching, according to Dewey, often uncritically accept this everyday reality in their schools and concentrate their efforts on finding the most effective and efficient means to solve problems that have largely been defined for them by this collective code. These teachers often lose sight of the fact that their everyday reality is only one of many possible alternatives, a selection from a larger universe of possibilities. They often lose sight of the purposes and ends toward which they are working and become merely the agents of others. They forget that there is more than one way to frame every problem. Unreflective teachers automatically accept the view of the problem that is the commonly accepted one in a given situation.

Dewey defines reflective action as that which involves active, persistent, and careful consideration of any belief or practice in light of the reasons that support it and the further consequences to which it leads. According to Dewey, reflection does not consist of a series of steps or procedures to be used by teachers. Rather it is a holistic way of meeting and responding to problems, a way of being as a teacher. Reflective action is also a process that involves more than logical and rational problem-solving processes. Reflection involves intuition, emotion, and passion and is not something that can be neatly packaged as a set of techniques for teachers to use (Greene, 1986).

This holistic feature needs to be stressed. Many of us go into teaching because we think and feel strongly about improving the conditions for children's learning. We believe that we can make a difference in students' lives. When we reflect about students in our classrooms, we need to listen to and accept many sources of understanding. We need to utilize both our heads and our hearts, our reasoning capacities and our emotional insights. The craft of teaching has many sources and resources. We should neither discount nor unduly limit those tools that serve as the sources and resources of our craft. In reflective action, in contrast to routine action, reason and emotion are engaged. And for Dewey three attitudes are integral to reflective action: openmindedness, responsibility, and wholeheartedness.

Openmindedness

Openmindedness is an active desire to listen to more sides than one, to give full attention to alternative possibilities, and to recognize the possibility of error even in beliefs that are dearest to us. Teachers who are openminded are continually examining the rationales that underlie what is taken as natural and right, and take pains to seek out conflicting evidence. Reflective teachers are continually asking themselves why they are doing what they are doing.

Dewey's conception of openmindedness can be usefully compared with the sociologist C. Wright Mills' conceptions of beliefs and believers. Mills argued that there are three types of believers: vulgar, sophisticated, and critical (Valli, 1993). Vulgar believers have no interest in listening to opposing arguments or in analyzing their own beliefs and operate only according to slogans and stereotypes. Sophisticated believers, on the other hand, are interested in knowing opposing points of view, but only for the purpose of refuting them. Sophisticated believers are still not open to the possibility that their own belief system might be flawed. Critical believers, however, are willing to enter sympathetically into opposing points of view because they realize that all belief systems have weaknesses and can be strengthened by the confrontation with different beliefs. Dewey's conception of openmindedness is akin to Mills' understanding of critical believers. Openmindedness accepts the strengths and limitations of distinct ways of looking at students, learning, and schooling. An individual who is openminded does not attempt to hold the banner for one and only one perspective, and he or she does not look to other perspectives with argumentative delight. Instead an openminded individual listens to and accepts the strengths and weaknesses of his or her own and others' perspectives.

Responsibility

The second precondition for reflective action, according to Dewey, an attitude of responsibility, involves careful consideration of the consequences to which an action leads. Responsible teachers ask themselves why they are doing what they are doing in a way that goes beyond questions of immediate utility (i.e., does it work) to consider the ways in which it is working, why it is working, and for whom it is working.

This attitude of responsibility involves thinking about at least three kinds of consequences of one's teaching: (a) personal consequences—the effects of one's teaching on pupil self-concepts; (b) academic consequences—the effects of one's teaching on pupils' intellectual development; and (c) social and political consequences—the projected effects of one's teaching on the life chances of various pupils. (For a further elaboration of these three points see Pollard & Tann, 1993.)

Responsibility for reflection involves an examination of these issues and more. It is not simply addressing the narrow question of whether one's objectives or goals have been met. This attitude of responsibility has to involve reflection about the unexpected outcomes of teaching because teaching, even under the best of conditions, always involves unintended as well as intended outcomes. Reflective teachers evaluate their teaching by asking the broader questions, "are the results good, for whom and in what ways," not merely "have my objectives been met?"

Wholeheartedness

The third attitude necessary for reflection, according to Dewey, is whole-heartedness. By this he meant that openmindedness and responsibility must be central components in the professional life of the reflective teacher. Teachers who are wholehearted regularly examine their own assumptions and beliefs and the results of their actions and approach all situations with the attitude that they can learn something new. As teachers, they continually strive to understand their own teaching and the way in which it impacts their students and they make deliberate efforts to see situations from different perspectives. Possession of these attitudes of openmindedness, responsibility, and wholeheartedness, together with a command of skills of inquiry such as observation and analysis, define for Dewey a teacher who is reflective. Reflection:

> emancipates us from merely impulsive and routine activity ... enables us to direct our actions with foresight and to plan according to ends in view of purposes of which we are aware. It enables us to know what we are about when we act. (Dewey, 1933, p. 17)

However, knowing what we are about when we act does not ensure that we always are successful, that we engage and touch all of our students, or that we walk around filled to the brim with special insights into ourselves, our students, or the school community. Reflective teachers are fallible teachers. Reflective teachers are not some sort of special superwomen or supermen. Reflective teachers are simply and unabashedly committed to the education of all of their students and to their own education as teachers. When they make mistakes they are not overly harsh toward themselves. They move on. The dispositions of openmindedness, responsibility, and wholeheartedness are dispositions that push one toward a critical and supportive examination of one's teaching.

- As a student, could you discern these qualities in your teachers? As a beginning or practicing teacher, can you see these qualities in yourself or in your colleagues?
- In what ways might the structure of classrooms and schools contribute to and/or discourage teacher reflectivity?

REFLECTION AND THE PRESSURES OF TEACHING

- Some argue that teaching is too demanding and complex to expect teachers to be very reflective about their work? What do you think?

Dewey's ideas regarding the concept of reflective teaching might seem to be somewhat idealized and divorced from the complex and uncertain reality of teachers' work. After all, who, given the choice, wouldn't want to be considered a reflective teacher. But what about the world of the classroom where things are busy and complicated? It has frequently been pointed out that classrooms are fast-paced and unpredictable environments where teachers must make hundreds of spontaneous decisions each day. There are numerous institutional constraints that increase the complexity of teachers' work such as the lack of time, high teacher–pupil ratios, and pressure to cover a required and broadly defined curriculum. The point is often made that teachers don't have the time to reflect because of the necessity for them to act quickly in this fast paced and constraining classroom environment.

Is this an adequate criticism of reflective teaching? We don't think so. Dewey was not suggesting that reflective teachers reflect about everything all of the time. Obviously, a purely contemplative stance for teachers is not appropriate or possible. What Dewey was talking about is a balance between reflection and routine, between thought and action. A certain amount of routine is of course necessary to keep our lives manageable. Without some routine, without some secure assumptions, we would be unable to act or react. Some sort of balance needs to be achieved between our reliance on and our examination of those assumptions and routines that guide us daily. Dewey was arguing that teachers need to seek a balance between the arrogance that blindly rejects what is commonly accepted as truth, and the servility that blindly receives this truth. For Dewey, it is blindness to act without questioning our received truths and it is arrogance to question everything all of the time. Certainly there is such a thing as too much thinking, such as when a person finds it difficult to reach any definite conclusion and wanders helplessly among the multitude of choices presented by a situation. But to say that the busy and complicated world of the classroom makes it impossible for teachers to be reflective is to distort Dewey's ideas about reflective practice.

The issue here is this: whether and to what degree teachers' decisions are primarily directed by others, by impulse, or by convention without coming to a conscious decision that they are the right things to do or, on the other hand, whether they are doing things that they have consciously decided they want to be doing. Many who have embraced Dewey's ideas about teachers as reflective practitioners, view teachers as educational leaders who can learn from others, and even take direction at times, but in the end who are not subservient to those removed from the classroom. The late Lawrence Stenhouse of the United Kingdom very clearly described this tension between external and internal direction in the lives of teachers and takes a position in support of the kind of reflective action that Dewey promoted.

> Good teachers are necessarily autonomous in professional judgment. They do not need to be told what to do. They are not professionally the dependents of researchers or superintendents, of innovators, of supervisors. This does not mean that they do not welcome access to ideas created by other people at other places or in other times. Nor do they reject advice, consultancy or support. But they do know that ideas and people are not much real use until they are digested to the point where they are subject to the teacher's own judgment. In short, it is the task of all educators outside of the classroom to serve teachers. For only they are in the position to create good teaching. (Ruddick & Hopkins, 1985, p. 104)

- Think about this statement. Do you agree or disagree? What specific implications do you see in Stenhouse's view for your own teaching?

Historically and conceptually, Dewey provides the foundation for our understanding of reflective teaching. His ideas form an important part of our understanding of reflective teaching. The notions of openmindedness, responsibility, and wholeheartedness are key features of a reflective teacher. But if we stopped here with Dewey's elaboration, we would not have a very detailed understanding of reflection. Dewey is helpful because his elaboration points us in the right direction. But others, especially Schon, have embraced the notion of reflective practice and have helped us to see more clearly how it can operate in our daily work lives.

SCHON: "REFLECTION-ON-ACTION" AND "REFLECTION-IN-ACTION"

Another influential thinker in the reflective practice movement has been Schon of the Massachusetts Institute of Technology (MIT). In his widely cited book, *The Reflective Practitioner*, Schon (1983) presents a very thorough critique of the technical rationality that has dominated professional practice throughout most of the 20th century. We do not dwell on his critique here, but rather focus on his understanding of reflective practice. According to Schon, reflection can be seen in two time frames. First, reflection can occur before and after an action—and this is what he has called *reflection-on-action*. In teaching, reflection-on-action occurs before a lesson when we plan for and think about our lesson and after instruction when we consider what occurred. And reflection can also occur during the action as well. Frequently, practitioners have reflective conversations with the situations while they are engaged in their efforts. That is, practitioners attempt to frame and solve problems on the spot. When teaching, we frequently encounter an unexpected student reaction or perception. While we are teaching we attempt to adjust our instruction to take into account these reactions. Schon called this *reflection-in-action*. According to Schon, reflective practitioners reflect both "in" and "on" action.

These concepts of reflection-in- and on-action are based on a view of knowledge and an understanding of theory and practice that are very different from the traditional ones that have dominated educational discourse. In the traditional view of technical rationality, there is a separation between theory and practice that must somehow be overcome. Here, there is the belief that theories are generated exclusively in universities and research and development centers, and that only practice exists in schools. The job of the teacher, according to this view, is to apply the theory of the university to their practice in schools. Little recognition is given here to the knowledge that is embedded in the teacher's practices, what Schon termed *knowledge-in-action.* Schon argues that the application of external research to the world of professional practice does not work very well in helping practitioners meet the important problems they face in the "swampy low-lands" of their work. He writes:

> In the varied topography of professional practice, there is a high, hard ground where practitioners can make effective use of research-based theory and technique, and there is a swampy lowland where situations are confusing "messes" incapable of technical solution. The difficulty is that the problems of the high ground, however great their technical interest, are often relatively unimportant to clients or to the larger society, while in the swamp are the problems of the greatest human concern. (Schon 1983, p. 42)

- Do you agree with this statement?
- What are the implications of this statement for teachers' relationships to educational research conducted in colleges, universities, and research and development centers?

According to Schon, there are actions, understandings, and judgments that we know how to carry out spontaneously; we do not have to think about them prior to or during their performance. We are often unaware of having learned these things. We simply find ourselves doing them. We are often unable to express this knowing in action. One way to think about the concept of reflective teaching is to think about making more conscious some of this tacit knowledge that we often do not express. By surfacing these tacit understandings, we can criticize, examine, and improve them. One aspect of reflective teaching and a form of educational theorizing is the process of articulating these tacit understandings we carry around with us and subjecting them to critique (Elliot, 1991).

- What are some of the things that you do automatically in the classroom without consciously thinking about them?
- If a student comes to you angry with another student or crying and upset—what is your first reaction? What are other reactions might you have? Do you ever react differently to students (or to their parents) depending upon their gender, race, or social class background?

In addition to the knowledge-in-action that teachers accumulate over time, teachers also continually create knowledge as they think about their teaching and as they teach. Strategies that teachers use in the classroom embody practical theories about ways of realizing educational values. The practice of every teacher is the result of some theory or other, whether acknowledged or not. Teachers are theorizing all of the time as they are confronted with problems in the classroom. Frequently these problems come about because a "gap" exists between their expectations for a lesson and the actual results. In many respects, a teacher's personal theory about why a reading or mathematics lesson did or did not work as well as planned, is as much as a theory as university generated public theories about reading education.

- Do you agree with this view of educational theory? Why or why not?
- What is an example of an educational theory that you hold about teaching that is based on your own or other teachers' experiences? How does it relate to the public theories about this issue contained in the educational literature?

Framing and Reframing Problems

Schon stresses the importance of reflective practitioners such as teachers framing and reframing problems in light of information gained from the settings in which they work. According to Schon, reflection-in- and on-action are the mechanisms reflective practitioners use that permit them to continually develop and learn from their experience. Schon argues that this process of reconstructing experience through reflection involves problem setting as well as problem solving because in real-world practice, as Schon (1983) maintains:

> Problems do not present themselves to the practitioner as givens. They must be constructed from the materials of problematic situations which are puzzling, troubling, and uncertain. ...When we set the problem, we select what we will treat as the "things" of the situation, we set the boundaries of our attention to it, and we impose upon it a coherence which allows us to say what is wrong and in what directions the situation needs to be changed. Problem setting is a process in which, interactively we name the things to which we will attend and frame the context in which we will attend to them. (p. 40)

According to Schon, as practitioners continue to reflect in and on action and to learn from their practice, the process of reflection spirals through stages of appreciation, action, and reappreciation. Practitioners interpret and frame (appreciate) their experiences through the repertoires of values, knowledge, theories, and practices that they bring to the experiences. Schon calls these repertoires *appreciative systems*. Then, during and/or after their actions, they reinterpret and reframe their situation on the basis of their experience in trying to change it. When teachers engage in this process of reframing, they look at their experiences from a new perspective. Munby and Russell (1990) describe the significance of this reframing process as follows:

> Reframing describes the familiar process in which an event over which we have puzzled for some time suddenly is "seen" differently and in a way that suggests new approaches to the puzzle. The significance of reframing is that it sets the puzzle differently, and it frequently does so in a fashion that is not logical and almost beyond our conscious control. (p. 116)

An example of this process is the situation discussed in chapter 1, of Rachel, the student teacher working in a multicultural elementary school. At first, Rachel defined the problem of six students' off-task behavior as one of dealing with disruptive students. After further thought and discussions in her weekly student teaching seminar that highlighted the racial and social class dynamics of the situation, Rachel began to consider these cultural dynamics and to reframe her task as one of providing more culturally relevant instruction to her very diverse group of students. Rachel began to name different phenomena as important: It was not simply the students but features of the immediate and removed context. She also began to frame the situation differently: The problem was no longer framed as one simply of student misconduct, but rather she began to look at the situation with an eye to the appropriateness of particular strategies with particular children. She then examined her own and her cooperating teachers' emphasis on student choice in light of the reframing offered by Lisa Delpit's (1986) article. As a result she "saw" the situation differently. Rather than implement a disciplinary approach that focused solely on the students' behavior, she thought about an approach that would facilitate and enable better student choices and use of time. For Rachel and other reflective teachers, the process of interpreting and framing our teaching experiences and then reinterpreting and reframing them is a central element of a reflective stance.

A part of this reinterpretation and reframing process is a disposition that some have described as an almost Zen-like "mindfulness." According to Robert Tremmel (1993), one of the primary qualities of Schon's notion of reflective practice is its emphasis on the need for teachers to give themselves up to the action of the moment and to be researchers and artists in the laboratory of practice, the classroom. Tremmel draws parallels between this close attention to the action in which they are engaged and the Zen Buddhist practice of mindfulness, which he defines as the ability "to pay attention to

right here, right now, and to invest in the present moment with full awareness and concentration" (p. 443). Tremmel argues that learning the art of
paying attention, not only to what is going on around one, but also within
oneself, is a necessary element of mindfulness and is a large part of
reflective teaching. He further suggests that mindfulness is a critical element in the problem setting and/or reframing processes.

CRITICISMS OF SCHON'S CONCEPTION

Reflection: A Singular or Dialogical Activity

Although Schon had a great impact on efforts to develop reflective teaching
practice throughout the world, his ideas have been criticized on several
grounds. First, Schon has been criticized for his lack of attention to the
discursive or dialogical dimension of teacher learning (Day, 1993). Although he emphasizes the reflective conversations that teachers have with
the situations in which they practice, and the conversations of mentors and
novice practitioners as the mentors attempt to coach the novices, Schon does
not discuss how teachers and other professionals can and do reflect together
on a regular basis about their work. Apart from the context of mentoring,
reflection is portrayed by Schon as largely a solitary process involving a
teacher and his or her situation, and not as a social process taking place
within a learning community. Much recent work on reflective teaching, on
the other hand, stresses the idea of reflection as a social practice and makes
the argument that without a social forum for the discussion of their ideas,
teacher development is inhibited because our ideas become more real and
clearer to us when we can speak about them to others (Solomon, 1987).

> Because of the deeply ingrained nature of our behavioral patterns, it is
> sometimes difficult to develop a critical perspective on our own behavior.
> For that reason alone, analysis occurring in a collaborative and cooperative
> environment is likely to lead to greater learning. (Osterman & Kottkamp,
> 1993, p. 25)

Developing a "critical" perspective on our own behavior requires the
dispositions of openmindedness, responsibility, and wholeheartedness that
Dewey highlighted almost a century ago and the collaborative and cooperative environment underlined by Osterman and Kottkamp. And implicit
in this type of collaborative and cooperative environment is the element of
trust. Teaching, when approached in the reflective manner that Dewey
recommended and Schon described, can be an intensely personal and

challenging endeavor. To be open to questioning long-held beliefs, to be willing to examine the consequences of our actions and, to be engaged fully in the teaching endeavor is certainly a rewarding but also a very demanding effort. To be engaged in this sort of examination with others requires that trust becomes a prominent feature of these conversations among and dialogues between practitioners. Without those companions, and without that trust, our reflection on our teaching will be severely limited.

- Can you think of an example in your own experience where participating in a discussion caused you to rethink and then change your position on an issue? Conversely can you think of a time when a group discussion made you feel uncomfortable and caused you to stop examining your beliefs or ideas? Can you begin to describe features or elements of either of these experiences that might help you to understand the enabling and disenabling features of those sorts of "critical" conversations?
- In your own experience as a teacher or prospective teacher, how important has the group context been in helping you to clarify and develop your beliefs?

Reflection as Contextual

Another criticism of Schon's work is that he focuses on teaching practice at the level of the individual without sufficient attention to the social conditions that frame and influence that practice. Here, the argument is that by focusing teachers' attention only inwardly at their own practice, Schon is encouraging a submissive response to the institutional conditions and roles in which teachers find themselves. Critics argue, and we would agree, that teachers should be encouraged to focus both internally on their own practices, and externally on the social conditions of their practice, and that their action plans for change should involve efforts to improve both individual practice and their situations. According to Israel Scheffler (1968), if teachers want to avoid the bureaucratic and technical conception of their role that has historically been given to them, and if they are going to become reflective teachers and not technical teachers, then they must seek to maintain a broad vision about their work and not just look inwardly at their own practices:

> Teachers cannot restrict their attention to the classroom alone, leaving the larger setting and purposes of schooling to be determined by others. They must take active responsibility for the goals to which they are committed, and for the social setting in which these goals may prosper. If they are not to be

mere agents of others, of the state, of the military, of the media, of the experts and bureaucrats, they need to determine their own agency through a critical and continual evaluation of the purposes, the consequences, and the social context of their calling. (p. 11)

- Do you agree/disagree with Scheffler's position? If you agree with Scheffler's view of teachers as needing to concern themselves with the contexts beyond their classroom, what kinds of challenges face that teacher?

- What obstacles arise when teachers attempt to "determine their own agency through a critical and continual evaluation of the purposes, the consequences, and the social context of their calling"?

- If you disagree with Scheffler's view of teacher in context, what is your preferred understanding of the teacher's role?

As former elementary teachers and now as university teacher educators and parents of public school students, we wholeheartedly support Scheffler's conception of the teacher's role. In fact, much of our work is motivated and guided by this "enlarged" conception of teachers' work. We fear that without such a conception in hand, the teaching profession will be demeaned and eroded by calls for others to dictate what teachers should do. In fact, we continually hear others proclaim that the experts need to tell teachers what and how to teach. Our alternative is not that teachers should dictate what should go on in the classroom, but rather that teachers and others who work in schools should work together with concerned and involved parents and community members to give direction and purpose to the education of a school's students. We can no longer tolerate or perpetuate the all too prevalent conception of teachers as existing "worlds apart" from parents and their community members (Lightfoot, 1978). Nor should we tolerate efforts to dictate what teachers should do in their classrooms. If teachers are to become positive and effective reflective practitioners, then contexts for collective action need to be created. Despite the view that such a conception is unrealistic, positive examples, although not bountiful, definitely exist. One such example follows.[1]

In the 1980s a group of elementary teachers in Milwaukee, Wisconsin joined together with a group of local parents to oppose a plan of the

---

[1] For other examples of school and community coalitions working for the achievement of the aims of education in a democratic society (e.g., educating all students to the same high standards), see the resource directory in Appendix A. The Fratney School example described here is connected to the Rethinking Schools group listed in the directory.

Milwaukee Public Schools to make Fratney Street School, their neighborhood elementary school, into an "Exemplary Teaching Center." The school
administration had wanted to staff the center with "master teachers" and
use it as a place in which they would bring in teachers who were experienc-
ing difficulties to learn the instructional techniques developed by Madeline
Hunter, an educator known for her "extensively marketed ... 'teacher proof'
instructional methods" (Peterson, 1993, p. 48). The parents in this working-
class, integrated neighborhood did not like the proposal as it meant that their
children would likely become educational "guinea pigs." It also meant that
their own proposal for a "two-way bilingual, whole-language, multicultural, site-managed, neighborhood, specialty school" would be ignored. What
ensued was a brief but intense 8-week struggle in which the "Neighbors for
a New Fratney School" won.

In an article outlining the history and the efforts to sustain *La Escuela
Fratney*, Robert Peterson (1993), a fifth-grade teacher at Fratney, identifies
four lessons that were learned in the struggle to run and maintain the school.
For our purposes, one lesson is particularly salient. Peterson maintains that
"parent involvement needs to be substantive and far reaching."

> It must extend beyond the pizza fund-raisers and volunteering for field trips.
> The central issues are power, resources, and presence. Do parents exert real
> power during their time spent in the school? Is there an ongoing, daily presence
> of parents in the school and in the classrooms? Are sufficient resources
> allocated to schools so that parent involvement can be adequately organized?
> The Fratney experience shows that this meant having parents and teachers deal
> with issues such as curriculum, budget, facility renovation, and personnel.

> Empowering parents in this regard is full of contradictions, however. Just
> because a perspective comes from parents doesn't mean it is right. In fact,
> throughout history, parents have played contradictory roles—at times fight-
> ing for the rights of oppressed peoples, at other times supporting book
> banning and school prayer and opposing equality and desegregation and the
> teaching of evolution. The bottom-line question is, what kind of politics are
> being promoted by the parents? How can a school community hear the voices
> of all parents and yet remain true to its mission to educate all students?

> Similarly, just because teachers are pushing something, doesn't mean that
> their proposals necessarily reflect sound educational policy. In urban centers,
> especially, where teaching staffs are predominantly white and children are
> mainly of color, the perspectives of some teachers and their organizations
> may be racist and class-biased. Teachers have a lot to learn from economically
> impoverished parents, many of whom have cultural experiences different
> from those of the teachers. (Peterson, 1993, pp. 63–64)

Earlier we noted that Scheffler argued, and we agreed, that the reflective teacher "must take active responsibility for the goals to which they are committed, and for the social setting in which these goals may prosper" (p. 11). Reflective teachers, when thinking about the learning that occurs within their classrooms, need to consider the various ways in which the school, community, and the larger social context enable or obstruct that learning. The Fratney School example illustrates that this reflection on the goals of learning may lead one to reasonably extend the responsibility to the school community. And at times, it may be quite reasonable to go further, to go beyond the school community and to examine the responsibility of local and state governments to particular educational efforts.

SUMMARY

Certainly Schon's conception of reflection has much to recommend it. His conception of reflection-in- and on-action and the accompanying spiral of appreciation, action, and reappreciation adds both texture and substance to Dewey's understanding. We would, however, agree that two features need to be added. First, although reflection can at times be a solitary and highly individualistic affair, it can also be enhanced by communication and dialogue with others. Second, reflection needs to focus not only within the classroom but on the contexts in which teaching and schooling are embedded. Recognizing those contexts leads to an understanding that decisions and deliberation over purposes leads to the inclusion of other members of the school community. But before we focus further on the nature of these extended communications, we need first to develop a more nuanced understanding of reflective teaching. We need to return to a focus on the texture and nature of reflective teaching. For this discussion, we have found the work of two Norwegian teacher educators, Handal and Lauvas, to be extremely helpful. In the next chapter, we focus on the contributions their work provides.

3

TEACHERS'
PRACTICAL THEORIES

In light of Schon's ideas about the appreciative systems through that teachers' perceive the world and that give rise to their practices, we next examine the nature and sources of teachers' appreciative systems (personal and practical theories), and the relationships between these often tacit understandings and teachers' practices. For in order to understand and direct our educational practices, we need to understand our own beliefs and understandings. So much of teaching is rooted in who we are and how we perceive the world. If a teacher is teaching in an impoverished rural or inner-city school and he or she believes that laziness is the basic cause for poverty, then it is likely that the teacher will see his or her students and their families as lazy or at least as potentially lazy. If a teacher believes that learning occurs best in situations where schedules are strict and order prevails, it is likely that he or she will require a certain degree of ordered behavior in his or her students. And if a teacher believes that the classroom should have the feeling of a "home," then it is quite probable that he or she will approach the classroom very differently than the previously mentioned teacher. It is likely that this teacher's conception of a "home" is highly dependent on his or her own upbringing, one that may be different from his or her students' conceptions. So, for these reasons, we turn our attention to teachers' beliefs and understandings and how to understand the relation between these understandings and their actual or likely practices.

Since the 1980s, increased attention has been given to the experiential knowledge that is embedded in teachers as persons, in their classroom practices, and in their lives (Clandinin, Davies, Hogan, & Kennard, 1993). Many names have been given to these appreciative systems that help structure teachers' work and their interpretation of externally generated theories and ideas: teachers' personal practical theories (Connelly & Clandinin, 1988), practical theories (Handal & Lauvas, 1987), teachers' strategic knowledge (Shulman, 1986), practical knowledge (Elbaz, 1983), and teaching metaphors (Bullough, Knowles, & Crow, 1992). Whatever name is used to describe the understandings, or theories, of teachers, it is clear that all teachers come to their teacher education programs and schools with beliefs, assumptions, values, knowledge, and experiences that are relevant to their teaching practice. Furthermore, it is also clear that teachers' practical theories, their assumptions and beliefs about students, learning, schools, and the communities that their schools serve, are continually formulated and reexamined when teachers engage in a process of action and reflection in and on that action.

HANDAL AND LAUVAS' FRAMEWORK FOR UNDERSTANDING THE SOURCES OF TEACHERS' PRACTICAL THORIES

Gunnar Handal and Per Lauvas (1987), two Norwegian teacher educators, have developed a very useful framework for understanding the structure of teachers' practical theories and have identified three different elements of these theories. They maintain that teachers' practical theories can be understood as the intermingling of personal experiences, transmitted knowledge, and core values. They add that although it is helpful to understand these various components of teachers' practical theories, it is important to note that these are, at most, helpful analytical constructs, and that inevitably these three components interact and intermingle to form a teacher's practical theory. That is, the meaning given to an experience is highly dependent on, but not determined by, an individual's central values, personal experiences, and received knowledge. For example, I can interpret a student's "outburst" as an example of his or her exuberance or as an instance of the student's inability to control himself or herself. If I value spontaneity, I might see the behavior as exuberance, but if I value self-control I might see the student as unable to control him or herself. Additionally, how one interprets and receives information is very dependent on one's prior experiences and values. For example, listening to an account of discovery learning as a part of an elementary teacher education science program may be perceived as one more instance of the highly idealistic nature of my teacher education program or as an example of a powerful instructional strategy: Much depends on prior experiences and values. But Handal and Lauvas note, and we agree, that in order to understand the potential texture and substance of teacher reflection, an understanding of these three categories of experience, knowledge, and values can be helpful. We begin with an elaboration of their conception of personal experience and then add to their understanding comments by Dewey on the role of experience.

Personal Experience

First, there is the personal experience that teachers bring to a situation. All adults have had a variety of life experiences, including educational experiences, that can potentially inform their work in the present—as pupils being educated, as teachers in various roles, as parents, and so on. In fact, as potential and practicing teachers, we have sat in classrooms for more than 12 years, and have accrued many experiences with teachers, other students, school rules and structures, administrators, and extracurricular programs. These educational experiences, along with innumerable other life experiences, form an "experiential" basis for teachers' practical theories. They are frequently the "stuff" to which we refer when we think about how we want to teach.

> For example, I (Liston) can recall my elementary and high school classroom teachers, the experiences I had in their classrooms, and how those experiences guide my activities today. In fact, in high school, I encountered three very different teachers with very distinct styles, styles that continue to affect me. There was Dr. Karl Keener, a rather formal social studies and civics instructor, whose Pennsylvania Dutch background seemed to create a distanced, and very polite classroom setting. His classroom environment was quite ordered and usually entailed Dr. Keener's lectures, some teacher-led discussions, and a great deal of note-taking. My experiences in that class taught me the value of inquiry. It taught me that social scientific inquiry could illuminate past and current social problems, and that this form of inquiry required a great deal of discipline and hard work. His teaching also taught me that a teacher could be very formal and at the same time quite personable. Dr. Keener touched a number of students in his classroom through his rigor and his expectations. He was a highly respected teacher, admired both by other faculty members and students. In his own very formal way he brought together the life of the mind and a concern for the students he encountered. And then there was Mr. Goodell, one of my high school literature instructors. There were times when he would come to class disheveled, and rambling on and on about some dream he had the night before. He would talk about the meaning of this experience and the import of such experiences for the members of our class. We

frequently had free-wheeling discussions and he frequently said what he wanted to say. He had few content expectations but he was a living force, one who thought out loud in a continual and frequently unexpected fashion. From Mr. Goodell, I came to understand the value of thinking about our experiences and thinking about them in a way that wasn't too constrained. I understood that such thought could be painful and difficult and I saw that such an approach did not always receive the support and understanding that it deserved—either from students or from other faculty. And finally there was Mr. Jones, a math instructor. Mr. Jones would frequently take the first 10 to 15 minutes of class to verbally berate or belittle a student whom he thought was too "radical" (frequently me) or criticize a recent school, local community, or national event. When he prattled on, he allowed very little room for discussion. Similarly, his math instruction allowed little room for independent student problem solving. As a student, I viewed his demanding approach as authoritarian and demeaning. Subsequently, as a teacher, I have shied away from airing my own political views in class, unless it pertains to the content under discussion, and I have encouraged students to both pose and solve problems. As a student, I had these and many other experiences with teachers, experiences that helped to form my understandings and expectations of what teachers could and should do, how one could or should act in the classroom, and the different types of learning environments that could be created.

The degree to which past personal experiences and the teaching experiences one encounters in a teacher education program contribute to the further development of teachers' practical theories varies considerably. In some teacher education programs, students are asked to observe teachers and students in public school settings and at times they are asked to teach sample lessons. There is always the possibility that these experiences and our past experiences as students will affect and shape how we approach and construe our teaching. Focusing on the experiences that prospective teachers encounter in a teacher education program, Handal and Lauvas (1987) state that:

> At a minimum, such teaching practice will give the "raw" experience of having taken part and performed a role in teaching situations. At its optimum, it will also give rise to an understanding of the situation and of the student teacher's own role in it, of why things went as they actually did; and even an understanding of more general phenomena in education, seen in light of this particular experience. (p. 10)

One can draw little or learn a great deal from one's experiences. The degree to which we learn from these and the manner in which they shape our practical theories varies.

Dewey argued that although firsthand experience in schools is critical to the education of teachers, not all experience is necessarily beneficial. He drew a distinction between experience that is educative in its impact on learners and that which is miseducative. He wrote:

> The belief that all genuine education comes about through experience does not mean that all experiences are genuinely or equally educative. Experience and education cannot be directly equated to each other. For some experiences are miseducative. Any experience is miseducative that has the effect of arresting or distorting the growth of further experience. (Dewey, 1938, p. 25)

Dewey (1904/1965) criticized the tendency in the teacher education of his day to place too much emphasis on the immediate proficiency of the teacher, and the lack of emphasis on preparing students of education who have the capacity and disposition to keep on growing.

> Practical work should be pursued primarily with reference to its reaction upon the professional pupil in making him a thoughtful and alert student of education, rather than to help him get immediate proficiency. For immediate skill may be got at the cost of power to go on growing. Unless a teacher is ... a student (of education) he may continue to improve in the mechanics of school management, but he cannot grow as a teacher, an inspirer and director of soul life. (p.151)

The experiences we have before we enter teacher education programs, those encountered within programs, and our subsequent work experiences as teachers provide a background of episodes and events that inform who we are and how we will think, feel, and plan as teachers. The degree to which we think about those experiences and the degree to which those experiences frame further events and enable us to continue to grow as thoughtful teachers constitutes, in part, our reflective understanding.

- Given Dewey's distinction between immediate proficiency and long-term development, where do you think that the emphasis has been (or was) in your own teacher education program?—On immediate proficiency? or on the long-term development of teachers?
- How do you feel about this emphasis in your program and why?
- How have your past educational experiences informed and guided your understanding of yourself as a teacher?
- What teachers stay with you and what aspects of their teaching affect you today?

Transmitted Knowledge

The second component of teachers' practical theories, according to Handal and Lauvas, is the transmitted knowledge and understandings communicated by others. In addition to what we directly experience ourselves, we also pick up and use other people's knowledge and understandings. We watch others act, we listen to and talk to others, we read books, watch films, live in particular cultures and subcultures, and so forth, all of which potentially inform our practical theories. In teacher education programs, we listen to university instructors and practicing teachers and we read texts in the foundations and methodology of teaching. For practicing teachers, Handal and Lauvas (1987) explain that this transmitted knowledge includes:

> The visiting teacher who comes to our staff meeting to describe his way of teaching a particular subject or topic, the course-book put together by experienced authors, the research report from an educational development programmer, the ideas about ways of dealing with pupils who have learning difficulties communicated by a colleague over a cup of tea in the senior room—all of these are sources upon which we draw to expand and "fortify" our "theory." In none of these cases is our own immediate personal experience in a practical situation involved, although relating to such experiences may make these contributions more meaningful and valuable. (p. 11)

As Handal and Lauvas relate, this notion of transmitted knowledge also includes concepts, categories, theories, and commonly held beliefs, that are transmitted to us by persons, the media, and the world around us. Just as is the case with personal experience, transmitted knowledge can have varied effects on teachers' practical theories.

- Think of some examples of transmitted knowledge in your own education for teaching. Are there any aspects of this transmitted knowledge that seem particularly powerful in helping you to frame and understand your experiences with students or with schools?

The relationship between transmitted knowledge and understandings and our practice is both simple and complex. Some knowledge is received as aphorisms or rules. There is the somewhat infamous teacher education maxim that stipulates: "Don't smile until Christmas." Here, the idea is that teachers initially have to establish themselves as authorities and that smiling and creating interpersonal relations with students diminishes one's authority. Other knowledge is transmitted as evidence for particular practices. For example, some have argued that discovery-based science instruction is most effective if the teacher initially frames the experience for the students (Bielenberg, 1995). Without some initial teacher introduction, the intent of the lesson may be lost on many students. And still other knowledge encourages a reexamination of some of our basic assumptions. Work by Shirley Brice Heath (1983) on culturally distinct uses of classroom questions has encouraged teachers to reexamine their use of questions and to examine how such usage affects distinct students differently. A student coming to class who is not used to indirect commands formulated as questions (e.g., "Why don't you put that pencil down?") may not at first understand the nature of that question-command, and look at the teacher confused. Heath's ethnographic studies help us to understand some of these classroom dynamics and the interpretations students and teachers give to those dynamics.

Gary Fenstermacher (1980), a philosopher of education from the University of Michigan School of Education has written extensively about the possible relations between research conducted by those other than teachers and teachers' practices. He describes further the three different relations just outlined. He writes that teachers can interpret externally transmitted knowledge: as rules, as evidence, and as schemata.

First, teachers can interpret external knowledge as prescriptions or rules for practice. This approach to transmitted knowledge is often encouraged by teacher education programs and by those who conduct staff development programs for teachers. Fenstermacher argues that this form of bridging external knowledge with teachers' practices should be rejected as a major strategy because it denies teachers a portion of their freedom to think and act independently.

- Do you find that your teacher education program has attempted to transmit rules of practice to you?
- If so, what rules of practice are being transmitted to you?
- How do you feel about this issue?
- Which rules do you find helpful and which ones do you find are not very helpful?

The second way of bridging external knowledge with teachers' practices is when external knowledge is used by teachers to test their beliefs. Here the external knowledge is used as evidence to help teachers accept, reject, and/or modify their existing beliefs based on their assessment of the external knowledge in light of their own experience and values. For example, some educational research has raised questions about practices that are very common to schools and could potentially cause teachers to rethink practices that are taken for granted as correct. David Berliner (1987), for example,

cites a number of cases in which research provides evidence that is counterintuitive and enables educationists and the public to further examine their
beliefs. He states that:

> One of these findings, which flies in the face of much current thinking, has
> to do with promoting students who have not passed the work of their present
> year in school. Schools are under great fire for what is called "social
> promotion." In this country, therefore, there is a wave of leaving back students
> who have not completed their year's work. The research, however, goes
> directly against this trend. The preponderance of research indicates that if
> there are two children who have not passed an elementary grade and you
> choose to hold one back and promote the other one, at the end of the next
> year the one who was promoted will probably be achieving about 15 percen-
> tile points above the one who was left back. Furthermore, the one who was
> left back has a lower self-concept and lower overall attitude toward school;
> he or she generally shows poorer personal adjustment as well. It is estimated
> that 1 million children will be left back this year because of the belief that
> children should not be passed if they have not completed their studies. The
> logic sounds fine, but the research does not support it. (p. 17)

Another example of counterintuitive research discussed by Berliner is
the finding that young children need high rates of success in order to learn
academic subject matter. According to Berliner (1987), "A good many
people seem to have felt that children learn when they are 'stretched,' that
some intermediate level of difficulty is needed. Perhaps this is because
adults seem to learn as often from their errors as from their successes" (pp.
17–18). But, Berliner maintains, the research on this issue is fairly clear.
Children in Grades 1 through 5 perform better if their homework and
workbook assignments "yield a success rate of 90 percent or better and ...
the questions asked in classroom discourse and recitation should probably
yield 80 percent or more successful responses" (p. 18). Some knowledge
can be used as evidence either for or against existing classroom practices.

Finally, teachers can use external knowledge as schemata (or organizing
frameworks) that can help them grasp in descriptive and explanatory ways
certain aspects of their work that were previously unaccessible. An example
of bridging with schemata would be David Johnson and Roger Johnson's
(1994) efforts to encourage teachers to think about cooperative, competitive, and individualistic goal structures as an aspect of their planning for
instruction. The concept of *goal structure* has served to broaden the way in
which many prospective and practicing teachers think about preparing for
a teaching activity by helping them to deliberately plan for individual,
cooperative, and competitive work.

Values

The third element of teachers' practical theories according to Handal and Lauvas is the *values* that we have about what is good and bad in life generally and, more specifically in education.

> The values in question may be of a more general ethical or philosophical nature concerning the "good life" (for instance that a meaningful life is preferred to an abundant life), they may be political values (like ideas about democracy, the distribution of values, freedom and the power of influence) or they may be more directly related to education (like equality of educational opportunity, the right to receive teaching in accordance with one's culture, and so on). (Handal & Lauvas, 1987, p. 12)

Focusing on values close to the classroom, some individuals believe that the teacher should be first and foremost concerned with the well-being and interests of the children. For these individuals, education should be child-centered. Others place a greater emphasis on the content, the knowledge, and the skills, that students are supposed to learn. For these individuals, education is construed as the transmission of knowledge and knowledge is seen as extremely important. And with regards to issues of cultural diversity, some educators believe that the establishment of a common culture, a core set of beliefs shared by all, is an essential goal of public schooling. Others maintain that such an emphasis only adds to the sense of oppression and disenfranchisement felt by those who are not part of mainstream U.S. society.

Additional examples of value-based reactions are not difficult to identify. Most all practicing and prospective teachers have definite value reactions to environments that are highly competitive or collaborative, and have attitudes and values about relationships of authority. Some believe that our schools are much too competitive and that such an environment harms those students who need just a bit more room and time to grow. Others firmly maintain that although we don't want to create harsh environments, we do need to get students ready for the real world of competition. Without competition, these individuals believe, standards of excellence will not be achieved. These values affect how we interpret and react to our experiences and how we look at and examine transmitted knowledge and, as a result, affect how we teach and interact with students and colleagues.

According to Handal and Lauvas, the three components of teachers' practical theories—personal experience, transmitted knowledge, and values—do not have the same weight or importance in determining the content of these theories. They argue that our values have a dominating but not singular effect on structuring our practical theories because we interpret everything through the lens provided by them. They write:

> Values, as we know from psychology, heavily influence our perceptions of things we experience ourselves, as well as what we perceive and accept in ideas presented by others. We sort out, delete and integrate, interpret and distort received impressions on the basis of what we hold to be good and right. A similar structuring effect on our new experiences ... is created by our earlier experiences.
>
> This leads us to perceive and use the knowledge transmitted to us from others in the light of what we value, as well as in accordance with the perspective created by earlier experiences. Thus the values we hold will—directly and indirectly—have a dominating effect on the structuring of our practical theories.
>
> On the other hand, we experience our own practical efforts very much in the light of structures, concepts and theories transmitted to us, in such a way that this may even lead us to change our values and beliefs to some extent. (Handal & Lauvas, 1987, p.12)

In contrast to Handal and Lauvas' view about the role of values in teachers' practical theories and subsequent practice, others think that due to the realities of schools and the actual conditions of teachers' work, teachers end up relying less on their own experience and values and being affected more by the institutions in which they work. Summarizing this view, Susan Rosenholtz (1989) writes:

> We may well argue that teachers' attitudes, cognitions, and behaviors have less to do with the individual biographies teachers bring with them to the workplace than with the social organization of the workplace itself—social organizations that are not characteristic of individual teachers but that teachers have helped to shape; social organizations that then have consequences for teachers' perceptions and behaviors. (p. 4)

Larry Cuban (1984) also provided a lot of evidence related to the constancy of classroom practice over time because of the way in which the structures of teachers' work (e.g., class size) have remained similar. We will not solve the disagreements over the relative weight that should be accorded to either teachers' practical theories or the social context in transforming teachers' practice. And we cannot come to any prior weighing of experience, knowledge, and values in affecting teachers' practical theories. But it seems evident that teachers' practical theories are an important element in their daily practice and that teachers' prior experience, knowledge, and values do affect that practice. And so as we think further about reflective teaching, it seems clear that teachers' practical theories would figure prominently.

- What are some of the key experiences in your life (including encounters with transmitted knowledge) that have influenced your current ideas about teaching and yourself as a teacher?
- What are some of the important values that underly your approach to teaching?
- What do you think are some of the main aspects of the nature of teachers' work that have accounted for the constancy of practice over time?

SUMMARY

Thus far, our discussion of reflective teaching has moved from Dewey's elaboration of reflective dispositions, to Schon's conception of the recursive process of reflection in and on action, and now to Handal and Lauvas' views of the components and sources of teachers' practical theories—their appreciative systems. In this elaboration, we have tried to move from fairly general typifications of reflection to the more particular and subtle features of reflective teaching. From the dispositions of openmindedness, wholeheartedness, and responsibility, to the conceptions of reflection-in- and on-action, and the framing and reframing of our experiences through altered appreciative systems, and then to the sources of those appreciative systems as being rooted in personal experiences, transmitted knowledge, and values, we have attempted to depict salient features of reflective teaching. The reflective teacher recognizes that a central source of his or her teaching practice is his or her practical theories, but is also sensitive to the way in which the contexts in which he or she works influence his or her actions. Reflective teaching entails a recognition, examination, and rumination over the implications one' beliefs, experiences, attitudes, knowledge, and values as well as the opportunities and constraints provided by the social conditions in which the teacher works.

Now we move on to other important features of reflective teaching. In the next chapter, we consider additional characteristics of the reflective teacher and attempt to bring teachers' theories and teachers' practice together in a conception of reflective teaching.

4

DEPICTING AND CONNECTING TEACHERS' THEORIES AND PRACTICES: THE STUFF OF REFLECTION

The notion that teachers' practical theories are formed out of the crucible of their experience, knowledge, and values is something that we should not forget. But at times, such analytical precision doesn't quite capture the feel of a teacher's every day life. In this chapter, we attempt to depict and connect teachers' theories and their practices. The notion that teacher's theories are, and can be, expressed as metaphors and images is one way to get closer to the reality of reflection. We do that in the first section of this chapter. Another concern about the reality of teacher reflection has to do with the "artificial" separation of thought and action, theory and practice. As we have already noticed, reflection occurs frequently both in and on action. In the second section of this chapter, we look further at ways of construing teachers' practices. Given that one of our main concerns has to do with the social context in which reflection occurs, we highlight the ways in which this social context can affect teacher reflection. And finally, in the fourth section, we outline distinct levels of reflection in an attempt to bring together both teachers' theories and their practices. Hopefully, these discussions bring closer together a conception of teachers' theories and teachers' practices within an enlarged understanding of teacher reflection.

34

DIFFERENT DEPICTIONS OF TEACHERS'
PRACTICAL THEORIES

In addition to the different *sources* of practical theories, teachers' practical theories also include different *types* of knowledge and can be expressed in a variety of ways. For example, Freema Elbaz (1983) claims that the practical knowledge (or theories) of teachers is concerned with knowledge of self, of the milieu or context of teaching, of subject matter, curriculum development, and instruction. Elbaz's depiction highlights the various types of knowledge that are entailed in teaching. It requires both classroom-focused knowledge and contextual understandings. This depiction of the content of teachers' practical knowledge is based, in part, on the notion of the "four commonplaces" of schooling (teachers, learners, subject matter, and context; Schwab, 1971) and suggests that it is important for teachers to be aware of the different types of knowledge that contribute to their practical theories and the variety of ways in which they can be expressed.

The practical theories of teachers are often expressed as images or metaphors as opposed to the logical-rational forms found in propositional knowledge. Propositional knowledge includes claims about teaching and schooling that can be said, more or less, to be true or false. Propositional claims are usually employed in arguments to convince others about what to believe or how to act. In contrast to propositional claims, it is said that images and metaphors are not frequently used for argumentative purposes and tend to function evocatively. According to Bullough et. al. (1992), "metaphors bear the images or conceptions teachers hold of themselves as teachers, their professional identity" (p. 7). And in fact Munby and Russell (1990), agreeing with Bullough et al., maintain that metaphors appear in the natural language of teachers as they talk about their teaching. Munby and Russell's claim is based, in part, on empirical observation and on a growing recognition that human thought is primarily metaphorical (Lakoff & Johnson, 1980) and that the knowledge-in-action embedded in teachers' practical theories can only be incompletely expressed through the sentences and statements of propositional knowledge.

Michael Connelly and Jean Clandinin (1988) view teachers' practical knowledge as emphasizing images and personal narratives. In designating the teacher's image as an essential element in teachers' practical knowledge, they point to an image as

> something within our experience, embodied in us as persons and expressed and enacted in our practices and actions. Situations call forth images from our narratives of experience, and these images are available to us as guides

to future action. An image reaches into the past, gathering up experiential threads meaningfully connected to the present. And it reaches intentionally into the future and creates new meaningfully connected threads as situations are experienced and new situations anticipated from the perspective of the image. Thus images are part of our past, called forth by situations in which we act in the present, and are guides to our future. Images as they are embodied in us entail emotion, morality and aesthetics. (p. 60)

In contrast to looking at teachers' practical knowledge strictly as a set of maxims or rules of "what to do," Connelly and Clandinin view this practical knowledge as a rich interweaving of images, experiences, understandings, and personal stories that guide and inform teachers' actions.

A number of teacher educators have recently examined the images and metaphors that prospective and practicing teachers hold about themselves as educators and have used metaphors as heuristic devices for helping teachers to become more aware of their teaching identities. They have argued that the reflection that occurs in the examination of personal teaching metaphors involves the process of reframing experience described by Schon. For example, Hermine Marshall (1990) argues:

Teachers may discover new perspectives and new solutions to the problems (of practice), ultimately improving the learning environment, by restructuring the frame through which they perceive a problem and generating alternative metaphors. (p. 129)

Some examples of metaphors that teachers have used to describe their approach to teaching are teaching as gardening and the planting of seeds, the classroom as a home, and the school as a community. Connelly and Clandinin found that teachers and principals act, in part, on the basis of their images and metaphors. As a result of viewing instruction as the "planting of seeds," one teacher derived practical guidelines for action. She felt justified allowing children to choose their own activities because she "knew they would learn in a more interesting way" (Connelly & Clandinin 1988, pp. 65–66). She also felt comfortable giving students ideas but not making them do the work. Another teacher who viewed the classroom as a "home," felt that classrooms and homes should have gardens where plant life can thrive. For this teacher, her home and her classroom were places where "growing things" became an integral part of daily life. Commenting on one particular principal, Connelly and Clandinin (1988) note that he had an image of

"community" in which the school itself is a community as well as a part of the larger community with which it is in dynamic relationship. This image of "community" is an expression of a narrative unity in Phil's [the principal's] life. ... The narrative unity is composed of threads that connect Phil's image of "community" to his ongoing narrative. The threads are found in Phil's childhood and school experiences in inner-city Toronto, in his experiences on the Toronto Islands as a child and as an adult in his first teaching experience in the Island School. (p. 76)

- What metaphor would you use to describe your own approach to teaching? Can you think of specific examples of how your teaching reflects this metaphor?
- Do you think that your teaching metaphor varies according to the grade level that you are thinking about, the particular school situation that you have in mind, or the subject areas that you might teach?
- What are some of the metaphors that you can infer from the behaviors of teachers in some of the other classrooms that you have observed?

It is our sense that teachers are capable of continually developing their practical theories, their images, and their conceptions of teaching as long as they continue to teach. Certainly, some teachers are more naturally inclined to be reflective or are in situations that encourage reflectiveness. And some teachers are more conscious of their practical theories and others have more developed and elaborated practical theories than others. But it remains an article of faith with us that the degree to which teachers articulate and reflect on those underlying images affects the degree to which they will be likely to examine and enhance their own teaching.

Teachers do differ in the content of their practical theories—they hold different values and believe different things (e.g., about themselves, the subject matter, and the context in which teaching takes place) regardless of how developed their ideas. As previously noted, teachers may employ quite distinct images and metaphors in their thinking about teaching. The educational literature produced by academics in colleges and universities has tended to describe these differences among teachers in terms of bipolar opposites such as traditional versus progressive teachers, teacher-centered versus learner-centered teachers, and so on. In fact, we began with a conception of the reflective versus the technical teacher. But the reality of teachers' theories is of course much more complex. Often teachers do not see themselves as belonging to any single category, but as holding theories of practice that locate them in several categories simultaneously. In chapter 5, we return to this discussion and provide what we think are helpful ways to think about some of the differences that exist among reflective teachers.

TEACHERS' EDUCATIONAL THEORIES
AND PRACTICES

Current thinking about the differences among the practical theories of
teachers reflects changes in the thinking of many teacher educators about
the source and location of educational theories. For example, Deborah
Britzman (1991) argues:

> We can consider the process of theorizing not as an isolated activity separate
> from the experience of teaching, or as a grand truth one attempts to impose,
> but rather as a lived relationship, grounded in the practical existence of
> persons and dependent upon the process of interpretation and change. ... The
> sources of theory, then, are in practice, in the lived lives of teachers, in the
> values, beliefs, and deep convictions enacted in practice, in the social context
> that encloses such practice, and in the social relationships that enliven the
> teaching and learning encounter. (p. 50)

Britzman is saying that teachers' practical theories are embedded in
social practices like teaching. This view of the embeddedness of teachers'
practical theories challenges the traditional view of the relationship between
theory and practice in teaching: about who practices and who theorizes.
Traditional teacher educators take the view that teachers practice but do not
theorize. The important point here is that accepting the idea of teachers as
reflective practitioners involves a recognition of the role of teachers in the
production of theoretical knowledge about teaching through their practice.
The process of reflection, in which teachers make more conscious and
articulate those practical theories implicit in their practice and subject them
to critique, can be considered a form of educational theorizing. This
practical and personal theorizing offers an insider's perspective on teaching
and learning in schools that cannot be gained from theories invented by
outsiders. The importance of teachers' practical and personal theorizing
cannot be ignored any longer as a key source of educational knowledge. It
is time, we think, to view teachers' knowledge as just as valuable as and
perhaps more able to capture the nuances and subtleties of teaching than
university-generated knowledge. And it is time to look at teachers' practice
with some understanding and knowledge of their theories.

One way of accomplishing this focus on teachers' practical theories and
their practice is elaborated by Gunnar Handal and Lauvas (1987) in their
account of reflective teaching. According to Handal and Lauvas, teaching
that integrates teachers' practical theories with their actual daily action

involves three levels of practice (see Fig. 4.1). The first is the manifest (or rather obvious) level of action (P1) where the teacher walks into the classroom, gives assignments, explains, asks questions, monitors work, and evaluates. The second level (P2), is planning and reflection where teachers consider why they do what they do in the classroom. This level of practice encompasses both aspects of reflection-on-action: teachers' thoughts and preparation before teaching about what they are about to do, and their reflections and activities after teaching as they try to learn from their actions. All too often, we view planning and reflection-on-action as located in the realm of "thought." But anyone who has taught and prepared for a class knows that such preparation involves both physical and mental actions and is an integral feature of their practice. The third level of teaching practice is the level of ethical consideration (P3), in which teachers reflect about the moral and ethical basis of their actions and raise questions about how or if their actions contribute to a caring classroom environment or to the enhancement of equity and justice. This level tends to focus predominantly on thoughts about ours and others' efforts.

It is worth emphasizing that both explicit instructional actions, the time spent planning those actions, and subsequent thoughts about those actions are all described as levels of practice. Handal and Lauvas maintain, and we agree, that it is important to view all of these aspects as elements of practice. Certainly, Level 1 includes the elements that we normally think of as practice. But they want us to see that teachers' actions and practical theories

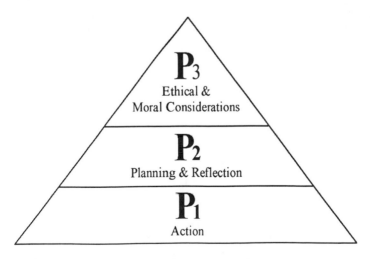

FIG. 4.1.   The practice triangle.
Adapted from G. Handal & P. Lauvas (1987) *Promoting Reflective Teaching* Milton Keynes
UK: Open University Press.

are inextricably interwoven in their practice. What we do at Level 1 is the result of previous reflections and actions found at Levels 2 and 3. Following are brief examples of each of these three levels of teaching practice.

Level P1

Consider two teachers: Cindy Fleener, an elementary school teacher who teaches math to a group of third-grade students, and Alison Harrison, a middle school teacher who teaches science to four groups of seventh graders.

Cindy has been teaching for 4 years at Kennedy Elementary School and she engages her students in group problem-solving strategies and activities. She is particularly fond of having her students work through problems in small groups, encouraging them to articulate to each other their understandings and rationales. For example, in beginning multiplication instruction she frequently gathers her students in small groups of four or five students each and poses problems of the following sort:

Suppose Mr. Ames purchased four posters for $2 each, four frames for $6.50 each, and enough glass to cover all four frames at a cost of $8. What is Mr. Ames' total bill?

Cindy then has the students discuss ways to solve the problem and she asks that they record at least two different ways of solving it. After the students work on these problems, they share both their procedures and their answers with the larger class. Cindy encourages students to question both the procedure and the answers in a respectful and helpful manner.

Alison has been working at Stevens Middle School for 6 years. Her science instruction for one class, like Cindy's math instruction, emphasizes problem-solving and experiential exercises. The initial lessons in each unit that Alison teaches employ experiments and real-life applications of the material that will be introduced. For example, during her lesson on geology and rock formation she starts the unit off with an investigation and examination of distinct types of rocks. She has her students work in groups of four or five to examine and discuss the differences and similarities among the rocks and she has them write down their ideas about how the various rocks were formed. She also brings in a number of fossils and has the students examine both the remains and the rock in which they are embedded. Alison gives her students basic outlines to help structure their observations. After these exercises, she assigns material in their textbook for both homework and in-class seat work and she lectures on these and related geological topics.

Level P2

Cindy approaches beginning multiplication and other key math concepts in this fashion as she wants to identify and make more visible her students' distinct ways of solving mathematical problems. She believes that if the students can see the various underlying rationales for mathematical operations (e.g., multiplication can be seen as repeated addition or multiple grouping), they will understand the material better. She also believes that if she can hear how her students are attempting to solve these problems, she will better enable them to see more clearly the way we do math. Although she is not against memorizing the multiplication tables she does want students to understand the operations that are the basis for those tables. At times she is frustrated with the parental pressure to simply memorize and move on. But so far she has resisted.

Alison enjoys watching her students try to figure out the various distinctions among the different rocks and to sort and "classify" the fossils. But whereas Cindy utilized these discussions as ways to make linkages to the mathematical operations, Alison employs this approach because the activities are fun and her higher ability students can both enjoy and "handle" them. Alison has noted that the students in the accelerated tracks can cover the required material in a much faster time than her other classes and she has found this "experimental" approach to be a way to hook them into the material that follows. In the subsequent readings and in her own lectures, she makes connections to comments and observations that students had made during the rock examinations. She tried this approach with one of her other classes and the students couldn't handle the relatively unstructured nature of the activity. So she has continued to use it with her accelerated group believing that it is beneficial for them.

Level P3

Cindy's approach is not accepted by some of the other third-grade teachers in her school. In fact one of them tells her that although her approach might be helpful and enjoyable for some of the students, it would be better for the students and more efficient if she grouped them according to ability. Mr. James tells Cindy that he thinks her approach is fine for the average student. But, he argues, the mathematically gifted student is kept from accelerating and many other students simply can't understand the mathematical logic behind the algorithms. Cindy disagrees. She thinks that although students may have different mathematical abilities, the differences are not that great and that at ages 8 and 9 all students deserve to see the reasoning behind the mathematical operations. She remembers being told that girls weren't good with numbers when she was a student and that never sat well with her. She believes that the only right thing to do is to assume that all of her students can learn the material and then to create situations where they have the opportunity to do so.

In contrast to Cindy, Alison does not believe that all students can learn equally or cover the same material. She believes that science is not for everyone and not anyone can become a scientist. For many years, Alison had tried to teach all of her classes in the same way with the same content. Then she found out that her "more talented" students really got involved with the hands on material and that her less inclined students would disrupt less if she kept them busy with the textbook and note-taking. A year ago, a parent had come in to talk with her about his son who had been interested in science until he started taking Ms. Harrison's science classes. The father thought that Alison could be more creative with the class but she explained that students at that level couldn't handle the hands-on material. He asked if his student could change his science class assignment and she arranged for that. Alison felt that if there was a mismatch (as in that case), the situation could be remedied. Generally, however, she found that her differentiated approach worked well, was generally fair, and certainly realistic.

These vignettes about Cindy and Alison illustrate a situation where on the surface, teachers are engaged in a similar approach to teaching. Once one begins to probe deeper, however, it becomes apparent that the two teachers have very different ideas about teaching. Also, when the specific types of students to be involved in the instruction are brought into the picture, these differences are brought into sharper focus. Although Alison holds views similar to Cindy about science teaching, she does not see her emphasis on teaching for meaning and understanding as applying to her work with her non accelerated track students.

- Can you think of other examples of teaching practices that might be engaged in for different reasons and with different ethical consequences?

As we noted earlier, we agree with Handal and Lauvas that all three levels portrayed here are instances of teachers' practice. Level 1 coincides with a more commonly accepted notion of practice, but all three depictions are part and parcel of and integral to what we call the practice of teaching. When utilizing such a view, it becomes easier to see how teachers' practical theories are part of their practice and how reflection entails an examination of both practice and practical theories.

THE EFFECT OF THE SOCIAL CONTEXT

Although teachers' practices are influenced in many different ways by their practical theories (e.g., how their values influence their choice of particular curriculum content or teaching methods), teachers' practices are also clearly influenced by the contexts in which they work. Rules, regulations, and mandates outside of teachers' control and influence often exert severe constraints on the freedom of teachers to act on the basis of their own practical theories. A good deal of literature has accumulated in recent years specifying in much detail the various ways in which teachers have been constrained by cultural and institutional forces, including attempts to micromanage schools by state departments (Wise, 1979), the influence of textbook companies (Apple, 1993), school district policies on curriculum, instruction, and staff development (Lieberman & Miller, 1991), the structure of teachers' work, which includes such factors as large class sizes, and little planning time (Freedman, Jackson, & Boles, 1983), and the forms of reasoning and rationality that underlie these and other efforts to control teaching and teachers (Popkewitz, 1991).

The so-called "second wave" of educational reform in the mid-1980s signaled a shift from rhetoric about controlling teachers to a concern for empowering teachers (Darling-Hammond & Berry, 1988). However, substantial pressures still exist that undermine the ability of teachers to exert leadership in schools and interfere with their own professional development. Even so, despite all of these pressures, teachers still interpret and give meaning to their situations in different ways according to their practical theories, and always maintain a certain degree of control over external influence efforts. The literature on education reform and school restructuring is quite clear about the way in which teachers have limited and at times have deliberately subverted the school reform efforts of external agents. For example, Seymour Sarason (1971) described in great detail the failure of the "new math" and other "teacher-proof" approaches to curriculum development to influence teachers' practices.

One example of the way in which teachers' practical theories influence teacher practice is the common situation where teachers in the same school who face the same constraints and opportunities posed by state, school district, and school policies make different use of their common situation. They will interpret the same reality in different ways, have different ideas about possible alternatives, and desire to do different things. It is very common, for example, to see in the same school both very traditional teacher-centered classrooms where most of the teaching is through whole group instruction and classrooms where students spend much time working independently and in small groups on various projects. Some teachers find ways to involve their students in activities that include but also go beyond what is suggested in curriculum guides, whereas other teachers only cover what is specified in the guides. Although external constraints are sometimes used by teachers as a reason why they cannot do certain things, there is always some freedom open for the teacher to influence external policies. There is no policy or external constraint so great that teachers completely lose the ability to exert influence in shaping it.

- Can you think of examples of teachers who are able to exert influence on their situations? How are they able to do this?
- Can you think of teachers in your own experience who provided their students with very different opportunities for learning in the same school?

For example, many states have policies that prescribe the amount of time that elementary and secondary schools must spend on the various content areas in the curriculum (such as reading, mathematics, science, history, art, and music) and dictate the use of assessment systems that are based on separate subject area exams. Although some teachers have used these kinds of requirements as reasons for not being able to integrate the curriculum across content areas and engage in multidisciplinary instruction, other teachers, facing the same state constraints, have managed to find ways to break down disciplinary boundaries.

Although teachers' practical theories are not the sole determiner of teachers' practice, they clearly play an important role in influencing the way in which teachers respond to the constraints and opportunities presented to them. No amount of conscious and critical reflection by teachers will by itself overcome external factors that affect teaching such as low fiscal support for public schooling and policies that limit teacher decision making. However, teachers' practical theories do have power to influence how they will make use of their situations. It will also influence whether and how they seek to shape and change external policies.

DIMENSIONS OF REFLECTION

In this chapter, we have examined the nature of teacher metaphors and images as one way of expressing teachers' practical theories, we have highlighted a way to conjoin teachers' practical theories and teachers' practice, and we have examined the effect of the social context on teachers' practice. Now we want to return to a focus on reflection and highlight the ways in which teachers' theories and practices can provide the substance for reflective teaching. And in this return to a consideration of reflective teaching, an important aspect of the process is the time frame in which it takes place. We have already mentioned Schon's distinction between reflection-in-action and reflection-on-action. Morwena Griffiths and Sarah Tann (1992), two teacher educators from the United Kingdom, articulated a framework of the temporal dimensions of reflection that goes beyond this basic dichotomy and describes how reflection by teachers occurs in five different temporal dimensions. They claim that teachers engage in cycles of action, observation, analysis, and planning at different levels of speed and consciousness, all of which are valuable and necessary to reflective practice. Furthermore, they maintain that if over the duration of their careers, teachers engaged in these distinct levels of reflection they would be better able to articulate their own practical theories, critically examine them, compare them with alternative theories, and revise them. We have found their analysis to refine and extend more fully Schon's thoughts about reflection-in- and on-action and in doing so provide a more developed approach to reflection and teachers' practice.

The first dimension of reflection, which is likely to be personal and private, is part of what Schon refers to as reflection-in-action. In what Griffiths and Tann refer to as rapid reflection, teachers reflect immediately and automatically while they are acting. A pupil asks a question and the teacher instinctively decides whether and to what degree to respond. A child asks the teacher to spell a word and the teacher automatically spells it for her, or sends her to find a dictionary or off to ask another student. Although all of the responses at this level of reflection are routine and automatic, not all teachers will have the same immediate response to similar situations.

The second dimension of reflection, *repair*, is still reflection-in-action, but here there is a quick pause for thought. Here, we would see such things as the teacher "reading" student reactions to a particular lesson and adjusting his or her actions, on the spot, on the basis of these readings. For example, at the end of a math assignment a fourth-grade teacher observes a student crying. Her automatic response is to go over to the student and find out what is wrong but then she recalls her last two similar experiences with this student. In the past two incidents the student was frustrated with his inability to complete the assignment, and when inquiries were made he became embarrassed and more frustrated. This time she decides to "ignore" the crying and see if it passes.

The third dimension of reflection, *review*, and all of the remaining ones are part of what Schon means by reflection-on-action and take place after the action is completed. Review, which is often interpersonal and collegial, can happen at any time during or after the teacher's work day. Here, teachers think about or talk over such things as the progress of particular students or groups of students, or the development of curriculum units and, as a result, existing plans may be modified.

In the fourth dimension of reflection, *research*, the teachers' thinking and observation becomes more systematic and sharply focused around particular issues. Here, the process of collecting information about one's teaching may involve a matter of weeks or months, although the process of changing plans for action as a result of this analysis remains the same. An example of the research dimension of reflection is teachers who are involved in the teacher research groups across the country that are sponsored by their school districts. Teacher researchers in places like Fairfax, Virginia; Madison, Wisconsin; and Philadelphia, Pennsylvania meet with their colleagues and staff development resource people throughout an entire academic year and develop research projects that inevitably lead to a conscious examination of important parts of teachers' practical theories, changes in teachers' practices, and sometimes to changes in the situations in which teachers practice.

For example, Pat Wood (1988), an elementary teacher in Madison, Wisconsin, engaged in a systematic action research project after observing that her students could not work successfully in small collaborative groups. She wanted to find out why this was the case and create a more successful and cooperative learning environment. Through a process of collecting data on her classroom practices and students reactions, through discussions with peers and colleagues, and with the help of others' observations she was able to restructure small group activities in which everyone "tried to cooperate more" and "work together better" (p. 145). Her effort is an example of action research, a form of research that is directed, focused and engaged in by teachers on their own practice.[1]

In the fifth and final dimension of reflection, retheorizing and reformulating, reflection is more abstract and rigorous than in the other dimensions and takes place over a space of months or years. Here, while teachers critically examine their practical theories, they also consider these theories in light of public academic theories. In one sense, advanced study and teacher

---

c

[1]Two excellent sources for other examples of teacher research are the journals, *Teaching and Change* and *Teacher Research: The Journal of Classroom Inquiry*. Both of these journals primarily contain reports of inquiry engaged in by school practitioners. See Appendix B for a more complete listing of sources of teacher research and teacher research networks.

rtification (at the master's and doctoral level) should aim at this retheorizing. Experienced teachers have found that some academic research helpfully informs their practice once they have decided the issues or problems they want to pursue. Teachers have also found, at times, that their reflections upon their practice inform and enrich the meaning of public academic theories. They have found that the time spent investigating issues, of retheorizing and reformulating these problems, to be a helpful corrective to a blinding immersion in the daily, weekly, and yearly dilemmas of schooling.

Griffiths and Tann argue that teachers need to reflect within all of these dimensions at one time or another and that too much of a focus on particular dimensions to the neglect of the others will lead to superficial reflection in which teachers' practical theories and practices are not questioned. All too often, teachers hear academics and researchers maintain that reflection that is aimed at retheorizing and reformulating is the only really worthwhile type of "reflection." And at times, university researchers argue that teachers tend to remain in the rapid and repair dimension of reflection. As elementary teachers and university instructors, we have found that all five time frames are needed (see Fig. 4.2).

1. RAPID REFLECTION	Immediate and automatic Reflection-in-Action
2. REPAIR	Thoughtful Reflection-in-Action
3. REVIEW	Less Formal Reflection-on-Action at a particular point in time
4. RESEARCH	More systematic Reflection-on-Action over a period of time
5. RETHEORIZING and RESEARCH	Long-term Reflection-on-Action informed by public academic theories

FIG. 4.2. Dimensions of reflection.

IS REFLECTIVE TEACHING GOOD TEACHING?

Now a teacher might engage in reflection in all five dimensions and be aware of his or her own images and assumptions about teaching, but one could still wonder if this "reflective" teacher is a "good" teacher. This is a complicated question and involves a number of issues that we cannot easily or quickly solve here. There is, however, an important point that should be highlighted. Let us begin with the fact it is often assumed that if teachers are more reflective about their work that they will be better teachers. That is, if teachers reflect and examine their basic values, are wholehearted and responsible in their concern for their students, are tuned into and have questioned the images that guide their teaching—then they are better teachers. Others reject this popular view, which they say all too often uncritically celebrates the results of teacher reflection and oversimplifies a much more complex reality. Here, there is the belief that reflective teaching is not necessarily good teaching and that uncritically accepting knowledge and action generated through teacher reflection is problematic, because under some circumstances, more reflection may actually serve to legitimate and strengthen practices that are harmful to some students. What seems to separate these two views is the degree to which someone can say of a teacher that he or she has critically examined the experiences, knowledge, and values that undergird his or her teaching, understands the consequence of his or her teaching, and can provide substantial justification for his or her beliefs and practices. Now the first group would say that as long as a teacher engages in that degree of reflection, that is all we can ask. The second group, however, would maintain that examinations and justifications are not enough. They maintain that certain key values, specifically the values of equality and respect for differences, must guide the educational enterprise and that we need to consider the actions that are taken in relation to the reflections. We tend to agree with value-based view.

Our conception of reflective teaching entails the critical examination of experiences, knowledge and values, an understanding of the consequences of one's teaching, the ability to provide heartfelt justifications for one's beliefs and actions and a commitment to equality and respect for differences. We think it is important to ask ourselves what, as public school teachers in a society that aspires to be democratic, what are our central duties and responsibilities? Minimally, we think it is essential that teachers be committed to all students' learning. But that is the minimal case. Certainly, the question of values in reflective teaching is more complicated than the celebration of a single value or value domain.

We have found the work of Amy Gutmann (1987) on what constitutes a defensible education in democratic societies very useful in helping us make determinations about what instances of reflective teaching to support and which ones to challenge. Gutmann argues that a commitment to a democratic way of life (a commitment that is embedded in the official rhetoric of most societies today) poses certain limits on what are considered acceptable educational actions. She argued that education in democratic societies honors three basic principles. This education: must develop a deliberative, democratic character in students; cannot repress rational deliberation by excluding certain viewpoints or perspectives; and cannot discriminate against any group of students.

An acceptance of these goals, leads to some principled limits on educational action. Gutmann proposes two such limits: nonrepression and nondiscrimination. If an educational action has the result of repressing certain points of view or perspectives that may be unpopular or not in the majority, or of denying certain students the reality of an education conducive to playing an active role as adults as citizens in a democratic society, this action needs to be challenged, no matter how much conscious reflection is associated with it.

For example, in one of the scenarios presented earlier, Alison consistently denied access to an education for meaning and understanding to her students who were not in the accelerated track. Although this stance may have been based on careful reflection on Alison's part about her previous experience, about her current context and externally generated research, it is not a position that we can ethically support as educators committed to achieving a greater realization of the goals of education in a democratic society.

Answering the question of whether reflective teaching is good teaching, in our view, needs to consider the degree to which the actions taken in relation to the reflection can be defended in terms of some notion of education in a democracy. This position creates the possibility that in some cases, reflective teaching can be bad teaching that denies the potential benefits of living in a democratic society to certain students because of their views, or because of their backgrounds.

SUMMARY

In this chapter, with the exception of the discussion on the worth of educational actions, we have focused mostly on the process of teacher reflection. But before we can make a determination that one's teaching can become better as a result of reflection, we need to look more closely at the substance of teacher reflection. Even though the reflective process may have been carried out very smoothly and is highly successful in helping teachers revise their practical theories and actions, we need to look more carefully at the thinking and the actions which result, the worth of the teaching practice. One way to begin to examine the worth of reflective teaching in more depth, is to focus attention on what it is teachers are reflecting about. In the next chapter, we consider the idea of reflective teaching *traditions*, which among other things, brings into view the substantive emphases in teachers' reflections.

5

TRADITIONS OF
REFLECTIVE TEACHING

TRADITIONS AND TEACHERS

Many efforts have been made in recent years to distinguish different forms of reflective teaching. As the use of the term becomes more widespread, educators are starting to realize that people are not necessarily talking about the same thing when they discuss reflective teaching. One way to make sense out of the vast array of orientations represented in the reflective teaching literature is to focus on traditions of reflective practice in teaching and teacher education in the United States. We believe that the historical perspective provided by a focus on traditions is necessary for understanding the present.

As we examined teacher education in the United States during the 20th century (Liston & Zeichner, 1991; Tabachnick & Zeichner, 1991), we identified five different traditions of reflective practice that have guided reform efforts in teaching and teacher education. These are the academic, social efficiency, developmentalist, social reconstructionist, and "generic" traditions. These traditions are very diverse. Each one focuses on different aspects of teaching expertise and different beliefs about what teachers need to emphasize in their learning and practice. Each of these traditions (with the exception of the generic approach) identifies a particular emphasis in the content of teachers' thinking. The academic version stresses reflection on subject matter and the representation and translation of that subject matter to promote student understanding. The social efficiency orientation

51

highlights the thoughtful application of teaching strategies that have been suggested by research on teaching. The developmentalist tradition underscores teaching that is sensitive to and builds on students' backgrounds, interests, thinking, and patterns of developmental growth. The social reconstructionist version stresses reflection about the social and political context of schooling and the assessment of classroom actions for their ability to enhance equity, justice, and more humane conditions in our schools and society. And finally, the generic tradition simply emphasizes thinking about what we are doing without attention to the quality or substance of that thinking. In all, except the last construal of reflective teaching practice, certain priorities are established, priorities that emerge out of particular historical traditions and educational and social philosophies (Liston & Zeichner, 1991).

It should be underscored that an individual teacher's approach to reflective teaching will most probably not fit snugly or exclusively within any one of these five orientations. This point cannot be highlighted or stressed enough. These orientations represent intellectual distillations of teachers' reflective practice and historical developments. We discuss them here as we think they helpfully highlight and organize ways of understanding reflective teaching. Generally teachers are not singularly "academic" or "developmentalist" teachers. As teachers we do not tend to hold to strictly defined orientations: teaching is rarely an "either–or" proposition. As living and breathing human beings, we are much more complicated than that. Although a teacher's priorities and circumstances probably lead him or her to emphasize certain aspects of teaching expertise, his or her practices will probably represent some pattern of resonance (and disagreement) with all four of the traditions.

It is our view that none of these traditions alone is sufficient as a moral basis for teaching. Good teaching needs to attend to all of the elements that are highlighted by the various traditions: the representation of subject matter, student thinking and understanding, research-based teaching strategies, and the social contexts of teaching. But it is important to understand that these elements do not take the same form or receive the same emphasis within each tradition. For example, technical competence in teaching when viewed as the excellently delivered lecture is not the same as technical competence that is sensitive to and tries to build on student understandings.

Despite the differences in the emphasis given to the various factors within these distinct traditions, many of the elements within these traditions are not mutually exclusive. In practice, significant aspects of the traditions overlap in many ways and each tradition attends in some manner to many of the issues that are raised by the traditions as a group. The differences among the traditions of reflection are defined in terms of the emphasis and priority that is given to particular factors within the traditions. For example, teachers more or less aligned with a social reconstructionist orientation are frequently critical of other traditions for failing to emphasize a concern for reflection about the institutional, cultural, and political contexts of schooling. However, it is not reasonable to conclude that just because a person highlights subject matter understanding that he or she is unconcerned with issues of equity and social justice. On the other hand, some educators lament what seems for them to be a "singular" focus of some teachers on issues of equity and social justice. However, it is often the case that these social reconstructionist teachers are also very concerned with teaching skills and student understanding. Good teaching comes in various forms. With that in mind, we examine and highlight the main features of each reflective teaching tradition. The following discussion of each of these traditions is accompanied by brief vignettes that illustrate the particular emphasis in each one.

THE ACADEMIC TRADITION

This tradition stresses reflection about subject matter and the representation and translation of subject matter knowledge to promote student understanding. Here, teachers reflect mostly about the content of what they are teaching, and although they pay attention to additional aspects of teaching stressed by other traditions (e.g., what the students already know and can do), the standards for assessing the adequacy of the teaching evolve primarily from the academic disciplines.

For many years, advocates of this tradition argued that all teachers needed to do to acquire teaching expertise was take a lot of subject matter courses in their preparation programs. It was believed that mathematics teachers who knew lots of mathematics, and biology teachers who knew lots of biology, would be good teachers and could pick up all they needed to know about the practicalities of teaching from a brief apprenticeship experience in a school. Recently, Lee Shulman of Stanford University and his colleagues, and a group of researchers at the National Center for Research on Teacher Learning at Michigan State University summarized a body of research that has clearly demonstrated that simply acquiring content knowledge as it is taught in most universities, is not adequate preparation for being able to teach. This type of "preparation" fails to provide prospective teachers with an understanding of key concepts in their disciplines or with the pedagogical knowledge they need to teach their subject area to their students (Grossman, 1990).

Shulman and his colleagues in the "Knowledge Growth in Teaching Project" (Wilson, Shulman, & Richert, 1987) propose a model of pedagogical reasoning and action, and of professional knowledge for teaching. According to their model, teacher knowledge includes three categories: subject matter or content knowledge (which has traditionally been emphasized within the academic tradition), curriculum knowledge, and pedagogical content knowledge emphasizing the links between pedagogy and academic content. Pedagogical reasoning and action encompass numerous aspects of teaching including instruction, evaluation, and reflection. The emphasis in this model is on transforming academic content through a process called representation, which:

> Involves thinking through the key ideas in the text or lesson and identifying the alternative ways of representing them to students. What analogies, metaphors, examples, demonstrations, simulations, and the like can help build a bridge between the teacher's comprehension and that desired for students? (p. 328)

Bill McDiarmid (1992), in summarizing work completed by the National Center for Research on Teacher Learning, and others, argues that several things beyond the mere knowledge of content are needed by teachers to be able to teach in ways that promote the type of deep and connected learning referred to by Shulman. Beyond knowing the content they are to teach, McDiarmid says, teachers need to know how to organize that content in ways that can help them provide their students with compelling and accurate explanations. They also need to know, according to McDiarmid, about the subjects they teach such as knowing how knowledge is created and the conceptual structures that organize and frame those subjects.

This approach to teaching is a good example of a contemporary view of reflective teaching, one that emphasizes reflection about content and how it is taught. It is a content-based approach. Although this conception does not ignore general pedagogical principles drawn from research on teaching, students' conceptions and developmental characteristics, or issues of justice and equity, the emphasis of the reflection and the standards for judging the adequacy of teaching evolve primarily from the academic disciplines. In our experience, many prospective and practicing secondary teachers find themselves comfortably aligned with this orientation. And we have found it helpful to explore with these teachers the values and understandings that undergird this reflective approach along with an exploration of the emphases in other traditions.

A Brief Vignette

Jennifer had taught high school math for 6 years and most of those years had been challenging and enjoyable. But this year something was different. This year, one of her students brought a gun to school and shot another student. This year, the larger world was brought into her classroom, and she was forced to examine why she persisted in teaching math to high school students. It had been a difficult year but now that it was coming to a close she thought she had a pretty good answer. Jennifer loves math. Ever since she was an elementary student she had found her math instruction to offer her both a way of thinking and an enhanced sense of herself. Mathematical thinking is logical thinking and logical thinking has helped her to understand complicated and messy issues. Logical thinking has helped her to clear up confusions. When as a student she was successful in her math classes, Jennifer felt a real sense of accomplishment. And others recognized her for those accomplishments. Jennifer believed that her experiences could be her students' experiences. She felt that they too could become enamored with mathematical problem solving and feel a real sense of accomplishment. As a teacher, she loved looking for ways to connect her mathematical knowledge, through her curriculum and instruction, to her students' initial understandings and backgrounds. In algebra she loved to utilize the search for the value of "x" as a means to explore story problems that seemed real to her students. She found the task of making the logic of math come alive to be a real challenge and a source of obvious satisfaction. That challenge and satisfaction is what kept her going and it was the reason why she would renew her contract for her seventh year. She might not be able to address or solve all of her students' issues. Who could? But she could certainly provide them with some real intellectual engagement and tools which they could use to clear up some of their own confusions about the world.

- What does commitment to subject matter really mean to you? What does it mean to be a social studies teacher? What does it mean to be a teacher of literature, etc.?
- What happens when individuals have different conceptions of the subject matter? What does it mean when some view the teacher of biology as an initiator of students into a way of seeing the world around them or as purveyor of central concepts and facts?

THE SOCIAL EFFICIENCY TRADITION

The second tradition of reflective teaching, the social efficiency tradition, has historically emphasized faith in the scientific study of teaching (by those other than teachers) to provide a basis for teaching expertise. According to contemporary advocates of this orientation, teachers should focus their reflections on how well their own practice matches what this external research says they should be doing. There is an assumption here that research on teaching has generated a body of knowledge (a "knowledge base") that can provide guidance to teachers. One contemporary example of this knowledge base is the framework for teaching provided by the late Madeline Hunter's staff development programs (Gentile, 1988) where teachers are expected to include certain specific elements in their teaching (e.g., advanced organizers) based on the belief that research has validated the relation of these elements to student learning. The assumption is that researchers have identified positive relationships between particular teaching strategies and student outcomes and that there is no need for teachers to accidentally come across these strategies when they could systematically learn them and then use them.

Sharon Feiman-Nemser (1990) identified two different strands within the social efficiency tradition: a technical strand that attempts to get teachers to closely follow what research says they should be doing; and a deliberative strand in which the findings of research are used as one among many sources by teachers in solving problems. In the first instance, the transmitted knowledge and experience serves as the major determiner of the teacher's practice. In fact, in this narrow interpretation the focus of a teacher's reflection is centered on how closely their practice conforms to standards provided by some aspect of research on teaching. We view this strand to be much too narrow and it seems much too similar to the technical view of teaching described in chapter 1.

In the second strand, teachers rely on their own practical theories and experience in making decisions, in addition to considering transmitted knowledge and experience. Here, teachers exercise their judgment about various teaching situations while taking advantage of research, experience, intuition, and their own values (Zumwalt, 1982). This more limited role for university research in the deliberative strand emphasizing teacher judgment is illustrated by Dorene Ross and Diane Kyle's (1987) comments about teaching as a decision making process:

> The limits on the appropriate use of teacher effectiveness research must be understood by prospective teachers ... the most important teacher behavior is the flexibility and judgment necessary to select the appropriate strategy for the particular goal and students involved. (p. 41)

Although this conception of reflective practice does not necessarily ignore the aspects of teaching stressed by the other traditions (e.g., academic content), the emphasis is on the application of knowledge produced by research conducted elsewhere.

A Brief Vignette

Eric had known for quite some time that a few of his particular teaching strategies needed to be overhauled. He had been teaching at the elementary level for 5 years and was beginning to feel that he could do a better job. One reason he had become an elementary teacher was the attraction of having a class full of students who could come together as a "community." He wanted students to work together in his classroom and he felt that when students learned together they could all benefit. For the last year, he had tried a variety of ways to gather his students into cooperative learning groups. He knew he had a knack for getting the students to feel like the classroom was theirs and that they were all part of "one big family," but when it came down to translating that feeling in specific learning situations, the achievement always seemed to elude him. So, that Fall he had signed up for a class on effective instruction at the local state university about 40 miles from his home. And the results of that decision were already beginning to pay off. He had found out that some of the research on collaborative learning indicated that: (a) the teacher needed to plan the group work with an eye to the "learning goals" of the lesson rather than with a concern for the social interaction among group members; (b) the teacher needed to know what kinds of group talk would serve as evidence that learning was being achieved during the group sessions; and (c) the teacher needed to be cautious when entering the group setting not to disturb the dynamics already in place (Meloth & Derring, 1991, 1992). In effect, Eric had found out that he had to be much more learning specific in his structuring of the groups. This had changed the way he approached and structured group time with his class.

- How can teachers adapt a particular research finding, when their own situations are different from the research context?
- How can research about instructional strategies be useful to teachers?
- What type of research knowledge would you like to have about teaching or schools?

THE DEVELOPMENTALIST TRADITION

The third tradition of reflective teaching practice, the developmentalist tradition, emphasizes reflection about students, their cultural and linguistic backgrounds, thinking and understandings, their interests, and their developmental readiness for particular tasks. The distinguishing characteristic of this tradition is the assumption that the natural development of the learner provides the basis for determining what should be taught to students and how it should be taught. Classroom practice is to be grounded in close observation and study of students either directly by the teacher, or from reflection on literature based on such studies.

According to Vito Perrone (1989), there are three central metaphors that have been associated with this tradition in the United States: the teacher as naturalist, the teacher as researcher, and the teacher as artist. The view of the teacher as naturalist is a conception of the teacher as a keen observer of child and adolescent behaviors and understandings and as a developer of classroom environments that are consistent with those observations. The view of the teacher as researcher emphasizes the role of the teacher in inquiring into his or her own practice. And the conception of the teacher as artist emphasizes the connection between creative and fully functioning individuals who are in touch with their own learning and exciting and stimulating classrooms.

One contemporary example of reflective teaching practice within this tradition is the work of Eleanor Duckworth at Harvard University. Duckworth (1987) has elaborated a constructivist view of reflective teaching that emphasizes engaging learners with phenomena, instead of explaining things to them at the onset. According to Duckworth, teachers are both practitioners and researchers, and their research should be focused on their students. Teachers should then use this knowledge of their students' understandings to decide the appropriate next steps for their learning. The important thing, according to Duckworth, is for teachers to keep trying to find out what sense their students are making of the classroom activities.

> The essential element of having the students do the explaining is not the withholding of all the teacher's own thoughts. It is, rather, that the teacher not consider herself or himself the final arbiter of what the learner should think, nor the creator of what the learner does think. The important job for the teacher is to keep trying to find out what sense the students are making. (Duckworth, 1987, p. 133)

This developmental conception of reflective teaching has become increasingly popular in recent years with the growing influence of cognitive psychology in education. Although it does not necessarily ignore issues related to subject matter, equity, and a knowledge base produced through university-sponsored research, the emphasis is clearly on reflecting about one's own students.

A Brief Vignette

Celia was amazed at what June had just shown her. That morning, three of Celia's second-grade students had pulled her over to see the pattern that June had made with the pattern blocks. It was an amazing pattern, one that took a rather complicated geometric design and reproduced it with various colors and in expanding proportions. Celia jumped on the opportunity that had availed itself and asked June if she wanted to copy the pattern down on the pattern paper and she did. The end product took some 3 hours to complete and it required of June a focused and sustained energy, a quality of attention that Celia had not observed in her before.

June had been one of those students who, on too many days, teachers don't "see." June had never created any real problems and didn't seemed to stand out in any particular way. She just seemed to be there. But today, June brought Celia back into focus. June had created a geometric pattern that was complex and wonderful and in the process had uncovered, for others to see, her own complexity and understandings. Celia wouldn't forget June and she would renew her own attention to the things that really mattered in her class-room—her students.

- What is the teacher's role in the developmentalist orientation?
- What is the teacher supposed to do with his or her observations of children? How can these observations inform or guide teaching?

THE SOCIAL RECONSTRUCTIONIST TRADITION

In the fourth tradition of reflective teaching, the social reconstructionist tradition, reflection is viewed as a political act that either contributes toward or hinders, the realization of a more just and humane society (Kemmis, 1985). In this tradition of reflective teaching, the teacher's attention is focused both inwardly at his or her own practice, and outwardly at the social conditions in which these practices are situated. It is a view of teaching that recognizes that instruction is embedded within institutional, cultural, and political contexts and that these contexts both affect what we do and are affected by what we do. A second characteristic of the social reconstruc-tionist tradition, is its democratic and emancipatory impulse and the focus of teachers' deliberations on issues that help them examine the social and political consequences of their teaching. Whose knowledge and whose point of view is represented in the curriculum knowledge in my classroom? How does the culture of my classroom compare to the cultures of the homes from which my students come? How might certain of my practices (e.g., ways of grouping and assessing students) potentially affect the life chances of my students, individual students, and particular groups of students (e.g., boys, girls)? Although this tradition of reflection does not necessarily ignore aspects of teaching highlighted in the other traditions (e.g., subject matter, student conceptions, research), the emphasis in this tradition is on thinking about issues of equity and social justice that arise in and outside of the classroom and on connecting the teacher's practice to social continuity and change.

> The activities of the classroom frequently carry with them as part of their own identity, meanings and values that are inherently political ... some of the most commonplace, seemingly innocent activities of the classroom, from segregating students by "ability," to discussing U.S. presidents in high school history, to "individualizing" the curriculum in elementary schools, promote political and ideological interests. ... Since school practice cannot be separated from larger social, political, and ideological realities, they (teachers) must be reflective about the full range of consequences of their actions. (Beyer, 1988, pp. 37, 39, 41)

The third and final characteristic of a social reconstructionist conception of reflective teaching is its commitment to reflection as a social practice. Here, the emphasis is on creating communities of learning where teachers can support and sustain each other's growth. This commitment to collaborative modes of learning indicates a dual commitment by teacher educators to an ethic where equity and social justice on the one hand, and care and compassion on the other hand, are emphasized. This commitment is also thought to be of strategic value in the transformation of unjust and inhumane institutional and social structures because it is felt that if teachers see their individual situations linked to those of their colleagues, the likelihood of structural change is greater than with teachers remaining isolated reflective practitioners (Freedman et al., 1983).

A Brief Vignette

> Sue had "stepped back" once more that morning to try to understand what had transpired. She had called Marlene and Jason, two colleagues, to try to put it in perspective—but she was still working on it. Yesterday, in an all-school assembly, the leopard mascot from the local NFL team had helped lead their high school pep rally. During the rally "Leprd" had gathered a male and female student side by side and somehow connected them with a scarf. When Leprd pulled on the scarf, out came a bra from the young woman's

blouse. After performing this magic feat, ole Leprd took a giant leopard leap and landed sprawled on top of a cheerleader. When he picked himself up he was noticeably excited. The whole experience was one that Sue found offensive. It was an assault on the two young women and an affront to all of the women present and to many of the men. It represented blatant sexual exploitation. Sue understood all too well that this sort of "play" was a feature of current society. She didn't like it and she had continually fought against it. But this was like a slap in the face to the two students and all other women at the rally. It was inexcusable in an educational setting. She immediately complained to the vice principal who made sure that the two girls were not harmed by the incident. And now Sue wondered what she should do.

In her literature class they had just read Virginia Wolf's *A Room of One's Own*. And so she decided to ask her class what they had thought of the pep rally. She knew that somehow she had to turn that experience into a "lesson," an object of examination, and a focus for their inquiry. Sue thought they could highlight what was harmful and thereby make the remembrance less painful and more empowering. She hoped that she and her students might be able to come up with a way to counteract that experience not only for themselves but for the rest of the school.

- When schools seem to support or reinforce social values that you find harmful, what is your responsibility as a teacher?
- Can teachers ever really be neutral in their classrooms?
- What happens when you, as a teacher, think students are being harmed but the students don't think so? What do you do?

THE GENERIC TRADITION

In the fifth tradition of reflective teaching, the generic tradition, there is an emphasis on encouraging teachers to reflect about their teaching in general, without much attention to how teachers reflect, what the reflection is about, or the degree to which the teacher's reflections should involve an examination of the social and institutional contexts in which they work. The central assumption that guides this view of reflection is the belief that teachers' actions are necessarily better just because they are more deliberate and intentional. In this tradition, how to get teachers to reflect:

Can take on a life of its own, and can become the programmatic goal. What they reflect on can become immaterial. For example, racial tension in a high school can become more or less worthy of reflection than field trips or homework assignments. (Valli, 1990 p. 9)

One contemporary example of this tendency to advocate reflection by teachers as an end in itself is found in the Ohio State University materials on reflective teaching that are used in teacher education programs through-out the country. Teacher educators have argued that teachers need to become more reflective about their work, without at all addressing the issues of content, quality, and the context of teachers' reflections.

> The point is that teachers who study teaching deliberately and become students of teaching can develop life-long assurance that they know what they are doing, why they are doing it, and what will happen as a result of what they do. Foremost, they can learn to behave according to reason. To lack reason is to be a slave to chance, irrationality, self-interest, and supervision. (Cruickshank, 1987, p. 34)

As was pointed out earlier, this kind of encouragement to teachers to reflect without identifying the things that teachers should reflect about or the quality of the reflection they should aim for, seems to lack both substance and direction. Reflection, like any other activity in which teachers might engage, can be done well or poorly and can be considered more or less successful depending on the substance of the teacher's goals (e.g., in relation to the aims of education in democratic societies) and to how well he or she achieves them. Teachers' need to subject their goals and actions to an analysis of their worth before their teaching activity can be considered good. The generic tradition does not encourage or readily promote these crucial considerations.

SUMMARY

All of the traditions, with the exception of the generic approach, highlight important features about teaching. Whether we are focusing on subject matter, student understandings, research principles, or the larger social context, we are reflecting on our teaching. Teachers, when they are engaged in this process of reflective thought, bring to the endeavor different mixes, different sets of concerns. It is not unusual to find that many secondary teachers tend to emphasize the content concerns of the academic tradition, while elementary teachers frequently highlight the students' understandings found in the developmentalist tradition. But these emphases aren't the sole concerns that guide a secondary or elementary teacher. In this chapter, we have elaborated in a rather singular fashion the key aspects of each tradition. In the next chapter, we portray the different traditions of reflective teaching with greater depth and complexity, combining them with the complex realities of teaching.

6

FURTHER EXPLORING
THE TRADITIONS

In this final chapter, we explore further the various types of valued teacher reflection, and do so in a manner that is closer to real life than the brief examples offered in the previous chapter. In chapter 5, we highlighted the central features of these distinct orientations to gain some clarity and understanding. Here, we offer examples of reflection that are rooted in a particular tradition but whose substance and concerns are not limited solely to the central issues of that tradition. By offering these "case study" examples, we believe the complexities of teacher reflection will become more evident. Certainly, there are teachers whose main concerns focus on the issues and values that exist within the academic tradition. But to identify or label that teacher as a "teacher within the academic tradition" may suggest a thinner rather than richer orientation. Each of the traditions deals with many of the same issues and rather than a set of issues "belonging" to a tradition, it becomes a matter of emphasis and degree. In one tradition, a particular concern will be a central issue, whereas in another tradition that concern will be an issue but not a central one. We hope the case studies that follow illustrate the complexity and the messiness of real-life reflection by teachers. And we hope that as a result of examining these cases, you the reader will begin to identify which orientation or orientations seem(s) to be central for you.

Following each case study, we raise questions, and after presenting all of the case studies we focus on the potential pitfalls and illusions that can accompany an approach to teacher reflection. Not all reflective teaching enables or empowers teachers as professionals or even aims to do so. After our elaboration of the case studies, we highlight those features that diminish the power of teachers engaged in reflection. Following that discussion, we conclude this work and look to the other books that are and will be included in this series.

IDENTIFYING ASPECTS OF YOUR OWN POSITION

An Academic Emphasis

The test scores on this semester's final exam were better than they had been for the last 3 years, but Jeff Lopez wasn't quite satisfied. He had the uncomfortable feeling that his students would be going into the second semester with some basic factual knowledge but with little understanding about and real engagement with biology—the study of life. Jeff had taught high school biology for the last 4 years and with each year, little by little, more of his students had placed well in their advanced placement exams. Eisenhower High School was located in a poorer section of town and had a higher proportion of students of color. For Jeff, the way out of poverty was through education. And education meant having a real knowledge and understanding of the world around you.

Jeff recalled his own high school experiences. He remembered sitting in Mr. Stallings' biology lectures and wondering not only how one person could know so much but also why he cared. After class, Mr. Stallings would take "young Jeff" aside and ask him how school was going. He always told Jeff that if he was going to go anywhere in life he needed to put everything he had into his education. Jeff never forgot Mr. Stallings' concern nor the time and effort he put into his teaching.

As a biology teacher, Jeff was a bit different from Mr. Stallings. Jeff felt that his students should not only be able to identify and classify life forms but should be able to think like inquiring biologists—to look at life forms and to understand and explain to others how "they worked." He felt like he had to come up with better presentations of the material, better ways to convey the complex processes and relationships that existed in the biological world. He knew it was his role to somehow convey that material to them, and at times he saw himself as initiating his students into the world of biological understanding. And for Jeff, this understanding had real power. It had intrinsic power but it also had a kind of political power too. The intrinsic power came from the sheer accomplishment of understanding and explaining the life processes around us. This accomplishment inhered the world with a sense of complexity and wonder that increased its special value. The political power came from the ability to use that knowledge to dispel misconceptions that harmed others. For too long, people of color had battled biological portrayals that depicted them as inferior. From the eugenics movement at the beginning of the 20th century in which "minorities" were viewed as biologically deficient and "alterable," to the gene pool arguments that were being bandied about at the end of this century—biology had been used to shackle, not empower, his own ancestors. He wanted to bring to his students an awareness of this two fold nature of the power of knowledge.

But the students' test scores, and probably even his own tests, seemed to miss the mark. He seemed to be emphasizing too much a kind of factual recall and not enough of the complex understandings that was the source of that power. He felt like he had to get at his students' conceptions and to link the material in ways that would convey better the biological explanations that he wanted them to understand. He thought back on his work with photosynthesis. His students could identify the major elements of photosynthetic process—they knew the role of chlorophyll and its interaction with light within the leaf cells. But he didn't know if his students understood this process as one of food production and the complexity of that production process. Certainly, some of the complexity would escape his students, but he needed to find a way to convey the notion of food production through the interaction with sunlight. And a key to understanding this process lay, he thought, in coming to see the complex interactions that could occur among cells, even perhaps the complexity of a single cell. And with that he thought of Lewis Thomas' work, *The Lives of a Cell*.

Thomas' work had a big influence on Jeff when he was an undergraduate studying biology. He fell in love with Thomas' ability to connect the study of biology to the larger world around him and Jeff thought that Thomas' work might just be a good place to start. He thumbed through Thomas' book and he found the analogy between the complexity of the human body and green plants. Jeff thought that this might be a way to make some of the connections he believed his students needed. In the initial essay entitled "The Lives of a Cell" Thomas wrote:

> But what of the other cells, sorting and balancing me, clustering me together? My centrioles, basal bodies, and probably a good many other more obscure tiny beings at work inside my cells, each with its own special genome, are as foreign, and as essential, as aphids in anthills. My cells are no longer the pure line entities I was raised with; they are ecosystems more complex than Jamaica Bay.

> I like to think that they work in my interest, that each breath they draw for me, but perhaps it is they who walk through the local park in the early morning, sensing my senses, listening to my music, thinking my thoughts.

I am consoled, somewhat, by the thought that the green plants are in the same fix. They could not be plants, or green, without their chloroplasts, which run the photosynthetic enterprise and generate oxygen for the rest of us. As it turns out, chloroplasts are also separate creatures with their own genomes, speaking their own language. (Thomas, 1974, pp. 2–3)

Beginning with something like this might, Jeff thought, help his students come to a better appreciation and understanding of the complexity and the workings of photosynthesis. Certainly, some of Thomas' ways of looking at a cell might seem pretty strange to his students, but he thought that he might have found a place to start. If he could get his students to see the role of chloroplasts, to see the complexity of that cell, then maybe he could get beyond the recall of photosynthetic facts. In fact, maybe the lessons on photosynthesis should become part of a larger piece on the wonders of cells. That might do the trick. And so Jeff began to see how he could restructure some of that material so that it would accomplish his goals of biological understanding: an awe of the natural wonders of life and an empowering knowledge that could help others.

- What does Jeff want to achieve with his focus on content, discipline-based knowledge?
- How is this approach to content knowledge different from an emphasis on knowledge as facts?
- In what way is Jeff's emphasis on knowledge as power similar to the social reconstructionist concerns for equality and justice? How does Jeff blend the two?
- What are your reactions to this approach? What concerns do you have?

A Social Efficiency Emphasis

Rose welcomed the new staff development focus on language minority students' learning. Ever since she had started teaching high school social studies, she knew that she was not reaching a proportion of her students. And as the years progressed, she knew that proportion was growing larger. She had always believed that civics instruction was a key component of public schooling, and she felt uncomfortable that she was not adequately instructing all of her students. She believed that all of her students needed to know about the structure and resources of federal, state, and municipal governments, individuals' roles and duties as citizens, and how to access and make use of public organizations. Each year she made sure that all of her students had a public library card and knew the public bus routes. For the Hispanic and Hmong students in her class, this seemed like a good start. But she knew that in reality it was only a very tentative start.

When Rose first started teaching, she imagined her classroom to be a kind of "elected deliberative body," a mini-congress, in which students would learn about state policymaking through simulating the deliberative process. In the intervening years, a different and less positive image had occupied her mind. For the last few years, she was beginning to see her classroom as an "educational holding cell"—a place where students were contained before they moved into the next institutional slot. She hated this image, but she had to admit it seemed pretty realistic.

Things were, she hoped, getting better. At the end of last year she had felt renewed when a number of teachers voiced their concerns about all of the language minority students that weren't being reached. And then the scathing reports in the local newspaper appeared that summer underscoring the teachers' apprehensions. It turned out that the drop-out rate of the Hispanic students was close to 50%. A vocal segment of the community expressed outrage. Rose and her fellow teachers believed something had to be done and so before the school year even started she and a number of staff members got together and created a plan. They believed they needed some outside help—they needed someone to advise them on the special processes involved for students whose primary language wasn't English. Rose and the rest of the Centaurus High School staff had just completed a 3-day introductory staff development session on CALLA (Cognitive Academic Language Learning Approach; Chamot & O'Malley, 1994). Rose thought that it might work.

What was intriguing about the CALLA program was that it was a research-based approach that focused on and integrated students' language development, content area instruction, and explicit instruction in learning strategies. This focus and integration appealed to Rose and to many of the other content specialists at the high school. The central component seemed to be the focus on instruction in learning strategies. The authors of the approach maintained that their own and others' studies had identified three major types of strategies that students can use to become more capable and proficient learners: metacognitive, cognitive, and social/affective. The goal of program is to "provide students with a menu from which they can select strategies they have found to be appropriate for specific types of learning activities and tasks" (Chamot & O'Malley, 1994, p.11). The strategies are keyed to particular content and language functions. For Rose, this opened up a whole new terrain of instruction—one that she had not through before and one that seemed to hold the promise of enabling her to help her bilingual students become more capable learners.

There was, however, a cost to the program. Like many staff development programs that focused on effective instruction, this approach did outline some steps that had to be followed in order for the method to work. There were many teachers in Rose's building who balked at being told how to teach and how to plan. On the third day of the staff development focus on CALLA when the steps were outlined, one could hear the audible grumbles and moans. But Rose thought that she needed to give the approach a try. She would look at how it worked with her students and see if the method was worth the planning it necessitated. And in reality, Rose thought, the steps were not that different from what she had been doing. But it was more structured. In the handbook it stated that:

> CALLA teaching requires thoughtful planning. The CALLA teacher not only thinks about the ways in which he or she will deliver instruction, but also thinks through how individual students will receive and act upon that instruction. ...
>
> Several steps are needed in planning for CALLA instruction. The first step is to select the content topic for a unit or lesson. ... Following content selection, teachers need to assess their students' prior knowledge of the concepts and processes selected. This information can guide the teacher in the next planning step, setting objectives for student achievement in content, academic language, and learning strategies. The third step is to assemble the materials that will assist the teacher in making the unit or lesson meaningful to students. Finally, the teacher outlines the sequence of instruction that will enable students to understand, remember, and recall the concepts and processes taught. (Chamot & O'Malley, 1994, p. 84)

Following this approach would certainly mean adjusting her normal proce-dures, but she felt that if it worked, if her bilingual students stayed in school and became more successful, then it was certainly worth it. She promised herself that she would try it until she found out whether it was successful. A schoolwide assessment process would be put in place, but she knew that she needed to find out how it worked for her students and herself.

- In chapter 5 we identified two strands of the social efficiency tradition: the technical and the deliberative strands. How would you describe Rose's ruminations?
- Throughout this work we have highlighted gaps between teachers' practice and researcher's prescriptions. How would you describe the interaction here between Rose's practice and the research-based CALLA program?
- What are your reactions to Rose's thoughts, situation, and predica-ments?

A Developmental Emphasis

Anna Levin is a first-grade teacher who last summer attended a lecture on a new program of mathematics instruction called Cognitively Guided Instruc-tion (CGI; Carpenter & Fennema, 1992). The basic theme of the workshop was twofold: first, teachers should spend more time finding out the strategies used by their pupils in solving mathematical problems; and second, children are often capable of solving much more complex problems than their teachers think possible. Anna had been curious about whether her own first graders were capable of the kind of problem solving she saw demonstrated by a group of first graders at the workshop and she wondered how she could elicit her own students' current abilities to solve several specific kinds of word problems involving addition and subtraction. Anna had always been intrigued by the way children thought and looked at the world. In fact, that was one of the big reasons Anna chose elementary teaching. She believed that if learning were going to occur it had to connect with the way her students' thought. And, Anna thought, she did a fairly good job of making that connection.

For the last few years, Anna had used her own version of a whole language approach for reading instruction and had found that it worked with many of her students. She had seen how the whole language approach honored her students' own strategies for reading and how it enabled them to become both competent readers and writers. They had become linguistically literate. She now felt like she might have a method that would work for her students in math. She now believed that she could help her students become numerically literate.

Anna felt that she was not the only one in her school who should look more closely at the CGI method. For some time now, Anna had been bothered by the differences between the boys' and girls' math achievement scores at her school. It seemed that by the third grade, boys consistently scored higher than girls on their math assessments. And by fifth grade, boys averaged half a grade higher than the girls. Even in her own experiences as a first-grade teacher, Anna was seeing girls leave her classroom in the spring ambivalent toward and at times frustrated with the math curriculum. She thought she might be able to provide a better foundation for all of her students.

So Anna had been trying out her own approach to CGI since the beginning of the year. It was now getting toward the end of February and she was delighted. First of all, Anna had been amazed with how many of her students could perform problems she thought were too difficult. She now had a much enlarged sense of what her students could do. She also found out that she could combine her own interest in word problems with the CGI framework for addition and subtraction word problems. With the CGI framework she could get a handle on distinct types of problems and come to see the distinctions in her students' strategies for solving those problems. In fact, to remind her of the power of this approach, she placed on the side of her file cabinet the following table that she had received during the CGI conference:

Addition, Subtraction, Multiplication, and Division Problems

1. Sybil had 12 stamps. She gave 8 of them to George. How many stamps did Sybil have left?

2. Sybil had 8 stamps. George gave her some more and then she had 12 stamps. How many stamps did Sybil have before George gave her any?

3. Sybil had some stamps. George gave her 8 more and then she had 12 stamps. How many stamps did Sybil have before George gave her any?

4. Sybil had 12 stamps. George had 8 stamps. How many more did Sybil have than George?

5. Sybil had 12 stamps. She put 4 of the stamps on each page of a book. On how many pages will she put stamps?

6. Sybil had 12 stamps. She wants to divide them so that she and 3 friends have the same number of stamps. How many will each person get? (Fennema, Carpenter, & Franke, in press)

These six story problems represented not only distinct types of problems but also the fact that children tend to approach problem solving in distinct and evolving ways. Her CGI workshop had taught her that initially students directly model the activity in the problem. For example, students tend to solve the first problem by creating a set of 12 items and then removing 8 of them. They tend to solve the fourth problem by matching and comparing a set of 12 items with a set of 8 items. And they tend to solve the sixth problem by dealing 12 items into four groups and then counting the number of items in each group (Fennema et al., 1993). The CGI researchers had found that these concrete modeling strategies provide "a foundation for the development of more abstract ways for solving problems and thinking about numbers that involve counting. … Children progress from counting strategies to use of numbers and symbols in an easily identifiable pattern" (p. 5).

In the last week, Anna was beginning to see the move from the concrete approaches to the more abstract processes in her children's thinking. That day she had asked her class to come up with strategies and an answer to the following problem:

Steven and his father had purchased 52 bushels of seed corn that day. The week before they had bought 58. How many bushels had they purchased altogether?

Anna then asked her students to take their time to figure out the problem and to be ready to report back to her, with number sentences, their strategies, and solutions. She had consciously limited their desk materials to paper and pencil supplies, excluding their regular unit counters and base 10 bars. To her surprise and amazement, many of her students saw 10s and 100s right away. As she walked around the classroom, she observed more than half of her students writing the following number sentences: $50 + 50 = 100$ and $2 + 8 = 10$ so $52 + 58 = 110$. And there were other variations. What surprised her was the number of students who were moving from concrete modeling strategies to more abstract algorithmic approaches—and doing so with understanding. And what she found so helpful was the way today's students' work would help her plan their lessons for the next few days. She knew already that Anthony still needed help with grouping by 10s. And she could see that Felicity and Charles were almost ready to look at the basics of multiplication—through seeing it as an example of repeated addition.

Anna believed that the CGI approach allowed her a research framework through which she could make sense of what she observed. She now could understand how her students approached these problems. She could see this for all of her children, the ones for whom math was a struggle and the ones for whom it seemed a breeze. And with this framework she could also figure out where to go and what to do next. No longer would she end the year with her female students disinterested in or unable to do math. With this approach, she believed could enhance all of her students' abilities.

- Anna has found an approach that recognizes and utilizes her students' attempts at mathematical problem solving. What are the developmentalist overtones here?
- What motivates Anna's child-centered orientation?
- How would you describe Anna's role as a teacher?
- What are your reactions to this approach to teaching?

A Social Reconstructionist Emphasis

Sandi knew, she really did understand, that lessons learned in the classroom were not always carried outside of school. But this was demoralizing. She had worked so hard with her sixth graders in their social studies/literature unit on diversity. She had stressed an understanding about other people's values, the need to create communicative bridges not walls, and the importance of and sensitivity to the language we use. But when she went to collect her students on the playground after recess, there they were playing a game that she heard her kids call "smear the queer"—a kind of one-against-all football game. It was almost nauseating.

She hadn't grown up as a radical or a "fire-brand," the kind of person who always seemed impatient and who forever harped on what was wrong. She had grown up in a family that cared for each other and with parents who had been labeled as liberals in a rather conservative community. But she wasn't like the mainstream either. She knew that. Recently, she had come to terms with her own sexual orientation and it wasn't heterosexual—she was a lesbian. And so seeing her students, her kids, play "smear the queer," struck both an educational and personal nerve.

In her unit on "Living with Diversity," she and her students had read some of the autobiographical literature that outlined the harm created by fear of difference. They had read Anne Frank's journals and 19th-century slave diaries. She had them hone their research skills through examining nativist reactions to U.S. immigration, noting the similarities and differences throughout the distinct waves of U.S. immigration. And she had them develop their written expression through interviewing and writing about individuals who had experienced various forms of prejudice. Maybe this was all academic to them, perhaps these lessons were simply another set of play-acting exercises that she, as their teacher, expected them to perform. But she thought her unit had been successful. Sandi had thought that she had helped them to become more skilled, more knowledgeable, and more accepting. Now she doubted if she had really accomplished anything.

Throughout the unit, Sandi had wondered if she should deal more explicitly with gay and lesbian issues. She had wanted to keep that issue at arms length because she knew that once she walked down that path she would soon find herself in some difficult situations. She recalled the fury and controversy that surrounded the Missouri high school social studies teacher who, during a lesson about the Nazi regime and the death camps, noted that the pink triangle identified homosexuals (Ruenz, 1994). He went on to indicate that had he been living at that time he too would have been herded up to a death camp wearing a pink triangle. Segments of that community wanted him fired. Sandi had no desire to make these kind of personal connections. She sensed that in her community, fears and misunderstandings about sexuality were too deep and irrational to confront. But here were her students, mostly boys, who had just engaged in a game of "smear the queer" and she needed to do something about it.

And so once they were seated in the classroom, Sandi decided to discuss what occurred. She asked them how recess went and then asked them what they played. A number of students responded with descriptions of their individual or small group play but no one from the "football" game offered up the name. She then described how she had seen Nathan, Jason, Peter, Brian, and a few others engaged in a kind of football game that she heard a few of the students call "smear the queer." Sandi then asked: "What does that mean?" There was silence. After a while, Nathan said it didn't mean much of anything except that whoever had the ball was going to get tackled by the others. But Sandi persisted: "Why the name 'smear the queer'?" Again there was silence.

Finally after what seemed an eternity Sandi asked: "So what is a queer?" After a bit, Brian answered that a queer was a "homo"—somebody who was a man who liked men, or a woman who liked women. Sandi then asked Brian if he liked Nathan and, turning red, he said that he did like Nathan but he was talking about homosexuals who really liked their same sex, they had sex with them. Now Sandi knew she was getting to the heart of the issue and so she asked: "Why smear them? Why play a game that seemed to be about hurting homosexuals?" And Jason said because what homosexuals did "wasn't right, it was wrong, and it shouldn't go on."

Sandi paused. She didn't know if she should go on, but she had gotten this far and felt she couldn't just end the discussion. But she could also tell from the tone of some of the responses that "reason" would probably not prevail here. There was an edge to some of the students' responses, an edge that made her feel uneasy and uncomfortable. Plus, she was becoming a bit angry and upset. So she decided she would draw a few quick parallels and then leave the matter for another time. She recalled the reactions to the Irish and Italians at the turn of the century—people thought they were "dirty and stupid." She reminded them of their interviews with people who had experienced prejudice, noting the pain, the anguish, and the lack of real understanding. And she stated that perhaps their reactions to homosexuals were similar to the prejudice they had studied just last week. But she could see that a number of them didn't buy her interpretation of the events. And so she decided for the time being to leave the issue right there.

- Some critics of social reconstructionism claim that this approach confuses educational approaches with programs for social and political transformation. Others argue that education is inherently political and always about change. Would you describe Sandi's actions as educational? Why or why not?
- Do you think it is the role of the teacher to have students discuss issues that are rooted in personal beliefs? Is it possible or desirable to always stay away from such discussions?
- The social reconstructionist agenda is one that is rooted in a democratic view of schooling and teaching? How do you feel about this approach?

REFLECTIVE TEACHING AND THE ILLUSION OF TEACHER EMPOWERMENT

The four traditions of reflective teaching outlined here engage teachers in a quality of deliberation that facilitates and further develops their professional lives. In fact, as we have noted throughout this text, a reflective teacher is one who is committed to his or her own professional development. But the reflective teacher "bandwagon" includes many variations. And although the reflective practice movement in teaching and teacher education has been closely associated with efforts to help teachers assume greater leadership roles in schools and to direct their professional growth and development, the way in which reflective practice has come to be used in many situations has done little to foster genuine teacher development. Instead, an illusion of teacher development is sometimes created that maintains in more subtle ways the subservient position of teachers. In this final section of the book, we briefly highlight practices that diminish, not enlarge, teachers' professional lives; practices that we have touched on briefly in different segments of this work but now believe we should highlight.

First, one of the most common ways the concept of reflective teaching is used in this restrictive way involves helping teachers reflect about their teaching with the primary aim of encouraging them to replicate in their practice the findings of educational research conducted by others, research that has allegedly been "proven" to be associated with effective teaching (effectiveness is usually defined in terms of student achievement on standardized tests). Sometimes this type of reflective thinking "training" encourages teachers to use their creative intelligence to determine the situational appropriateness of employing particular strategies, but often times, not. Assessing teachers according to how well their practice conforms to a standardized set of teaching behaviors as has been done in Florida with the Florida Performance Measurement System (FPMS) is an example of this illusory empowerment (Smith, Petersen, & Miccere, 1987).

The FPMS is used to examine a teacher's classroom practice according to how it relates to a set of 124 behaviors in six domains of teaching (e.g., planning, management of student conduct, organization and development of instruction, presentation of subject matter, verbal and nonverbal communication, and testing) that are allegedly based on research on teaching effectiveness. A supervisor using the summative classroom observation form that lists 39 of these behaviors checks off the frequency with which effective or ineffective indicators of the behavior are present in the observed teaching. For example, in the domain of instructional organization and development, a teacher is given a check in the effective indicator column for recognizing pupil responses and either amplifying the responses, giving corrective feedback, or specific academic praise. The teacher is given a check in the ineffective behavior column for ignoring pupil responses, giving general nonspecific praise, or for expressing sarcasm.

Although the FPMS and other similar programs use language that emphasizes the empowering effects of reflecting about an externally generated knowledge base of teaching and gives a message to teachers that they should engage in thoughtful use of research by engaging in problem solving, decision making, and so on, the fact is that this conception of reflective practice, one closely tied to the replication of a standard set of teaching behaviors, denies teachers the use of the wisdom and expertise embedded in their own practice. They are merely to fine tune and/or adapt knowledge that was formulated elsewhere by someone unfamiliar with the teachers' particular situations. "Theory" is still seen here as being produced only within universities and practice is believed to exist only in schools.

Closely related to this persistence of technical rationality under the banner of reflective teaching is a second phenomena. There are some reflective teaching models that limit the reflective process to a consideration of teaching skills and strategies (the means of instruction) and excludes from the teacher's purview ethical and moral realms of teaching. Here again, teachers are denied the opportunity to do anything more than fine tune or adjust the means for accomplishing ends determined by others. Teaching becomes merely a technical activity and important questions related to values such as what should be taught, and to whom are defined independently and relegated to others removed from the classroom. This instrumental conception of teaching practice that tries to limit teachers to technical concerns and to carrying out the values of others, ignores the inherent ethical quality of all teaching practice. The technical aspects of teaching are important, but they cannot be separated from the values that underlie them.

A third aspect of the current concern for encouraging more reflection by teachers is a clear emphasis on focusing teachers' reflections inwardly at their own teaching and/or their students, to the neglect of any consideration of the social conditions of schooling that influence the teacher's work within the classroom. This individualistic bias makes it less likely that teachers will be able to confront and transform those structural aspects of their work that hinder the accomplishment of their educational mission. Here the context of teachers' work is taken as given.

In encouraging teacher reflection about the social conditions of schooling, we must be careful that teachers' involvement beyond the boundaries of their own classrooms does not make excessive demands on their time, energy, and expertise, diverting their attention from their core mission with students. In some circumstances, creating more opportunities for teachers to assume leadership beyond their classrooms can intensify their work beyond the bounds of reasonableness, and make it more difficult for them to accomplish their primary task of educating students. It does not have to be this way of course, but it can, unless efforts are made to incorporate teachers' participation in schoolwide leadership into their work rather than adding to their work.

A fourth and final characteristic of much of the writing in the reflective practice movement is a focus on facilitating reflection by individual teachers who are to think by themselves about their work. There is very little sense in a lot of the discourse on reflective teaching of reflection as a social practice, where groups of teachers can support and sustain each others' growth. The definition of teacher development as only an activity to be pursued by an individual teacher greatly limits the potential for teacher growth. The challenge and support gained through social interaction is important in helping teachers clarify what they believe and in gaining the courage to pursue their beliefs.

One consequence of this isolation of individual teachers and of the lack of attention to the social context of teaching in teacher development is that teachers come to see their problems as their own, unrelated to those of other teachers or to the structure of schools and school systems. Thus, we have seen the emergence of such terms as *teacher burnout* and *teacher stress*, which direct the attention of teachers away from a critical analysis of schools as institutions to a preoccupation with their own individual failures. If we are to have genuine teacher development in which teachers are truly empowered, we must turn away from this individualist approach and heed the advice of teachers like those who were members of the Boston Women's Teachers' Group in the 1980s. These teachers argued that:

> Teachers must now begin to turn the investigation of schools away from scapegoating individual teachers, students, parents, and administrators, toward a system wide approach. Teachers must recognize how the structure of schools controls their work and deeply affects their relationships with their fellow teachers, their students, and their students' families. Teachers must feel free to express these insights and publicly voice their concerns. Only with this knowledge can they grow into wisdom and help others to grow. (Freedman et al., 1983, p. 299)

In summary, we find four practices that undermine the potential for genuine teacher development and we suggest four antidotes for each of those practices. First, we think it is harmful to try to focus on helping teachers to better replicate practices suggested by research conducted by others while neglecting the theories and expertise embedded in teachers' own practices. We maintain that a more interactive approach between teachers' theories and research endeavors is desirable and that a greater emphasis needs to be placed on teachers' deliberative abilities. Second, we find that a means–ends thinking that seeks to limit the substance of teachers' reflections to technical questions of teaching techniques and internal classroom organization, and which neglects questions of values and goals, is mistaken. Teachers' full deliberative processes need to be engaged and the guiding goals and values are central matters over which teachers should deliberate. Third, facilitating teachers' reflections about their own teaching while ignoring the social and institutional context in which teaching takes place is simply mistaken. Teachers teach students who live lives beyond the classroom walls, and schools and classrooms exist in settings that directly affect the type and quality of education that can occur. Reflective teaching is reflection on events that occur in and outside the school. Fourth, an emphasis on helping teachers to reflect individually and a neglect of reflection as a collaborative social practice unduly inhibits teachers' deliberation and their professional growth. Reflective teaching certainly can be a solitary affair but it need not be. In fact, teachers should be encouraged to talk to others about the issues, problems, and conundrums that they face.

CONCLUSION

We began this work saying that good reflective teaching came in a variety of "packages." But we also noted at the start that if teachers did not question the goals, values, and assumptions that guided their work and did not examine the context in which they taught, then they were not engaged in good reflective teaching. Reflective teaching entailed critical questions about the ends, means and contexts of teaching. In chapter 4, we stipulated that good reflective teaching also needed to be democratic in the sense that teachers must be committed to teaching all of their students to the same high academic standards. We remain firm in our belief that good reflective teaching is both democratic and self-critical. It is of course that and much more. But minimally it must be democratic and self-critical.

Hopefully, this text has enabled you to come to a more adequate understanding of our notion and your own notion of reflective teaching. We believe it is a helpful introduction. But, as we also noted at the beginning, this text is an introduction. The other volumes in this series are planned to help you further examine the practical theories, the experiences, knowledge, and values, that you bring to teaching and to explore issues that are pressing and pertinent ones for the teaching profession. The next volume, *Culture and Teaching*, highlights issues of culture and context in teaching and focuses on the multicultural curriculum debate. Other texts planned for the series include an exploration of gender and teaching, school reform and teachers, teaching in a language diverse society, and stories and teaching. These texts are and will be designed to encourage the kind of thoughtful deliberation that we view to be a part of reflective teaching.

Finally we offer a bit of advice. Teaching can be viewed as a job, as something for which effort is expended and money is received. We, however, view it as something much more. We think it is more akin to a calling—an endeavor to which a person ought to be passionately committed. In an era of worker exploitation, one that devalues the efforts of teachers, it may be difficult to get behind a notion of teaching as a "calling." But we think it is and we think it requires the kind of thoughtful deliberation that we have described thus far. We certainly don't think it is an easy task. It is a challenging one for all good teachers. And it is a challenge that good teachers can not ignore. We wish you luck in this endeavor and hope that your efforts will be rewarded and recognized. If they are neither rewarded nor recognized, please recognize your own efforts, continue to teach and reflect, and gather together with other educators and parents to claim your professional terrain.

Appendix A

A DIRECTORY OF GROUPS AND RESOURCES DEDICATED TO ACHIEVING GREATER DEMOCRACY AND EQUITY IN PUBLIC SCHOOLING

Boston Women's Teachers' Group

P.O. Box 169 W. Somerville, MA 02144. A nonprofit group that publishes Radical Teacher three times per year. This socialist and feminist journal on the theory and practice of teaching includes articles written by K–12 teachers and has addressed issues such as working-class studies, feminist pedagogy, and multicultural and antiracist teaching. Several years ago, this group also produced a slide-tape program, The Other End of the Corridor, which addresses the effects of the structures of teachers work on teachers.

California Tomorrow

Fort Mason Center, Building B., San Francisco, CA 94123; 415-441-7631. A nonprofit organization committed to racial, cultural, and linguistic diversity in California and to the building of a society that is equitable for everyone. Through policy research, advocacy, media outreach, and technical assistance, California Tomorrow stimulates public dialogue about the need to celebrate diversity as our most precious resource and racial equality as our only hope for becoming a just and great society. Publications include: *Bridges: Promising Programs for the Education of Immigrant Children*, *Embracing Diversity: Teachers' Voices From California's Classrooms*, and *The unfinished Journey: Restructuring Schools in a Diverse Society*.

Common Destiny Alliance

University of Maryland, College Park, MD 20742-2334; 301-405-2341. A national consortium of organizations and individuals committed to improving race and ethnic relations and to achieving educational equity. Provides research-based information related to race and ethnic relations and conflict resolution, teaching and learning in racially and ethnically mixed settings, and preparing teachers for cultural diversity.

Council on Interracial Books for Children

1841 Broadway New York, NY 10023. A nonprofit organization founded by writers and librarians, teachers, and parents in 1966. It promotes antiracist and antisexist children's literature and teaching materials and publishes (eight times per year) the *Interracial Books for Children Bulletin*, which analyzes learning materials for stereotypes and other forms of bias and recommends new books and resources.

Educators for Social Responsibility

23 Garden St. Cambridge, MA 02138; 617-492-1764. A national educational organization offering programs and curricula that support teachers in helping young people become actively and responsibly engaged in the world. Publishes a journal, *Educating for Social Responsibility*.

Institute for Democracy in Education (IDE)

College of Education, Ohio University, 313 McCracken Hall, Athens OH 45701-2979; 614-593-4531. IDE promotes educational practices that provide students with experiences through which they can develop democratic attitudes and values. It works to provide teachers committed to democratic education with a forum for sharing ideas, with a support network of people holding similar values, and with opportunities for professional development. Publishes a quarterly journal for classroom teacher, Democracy and Education.

Institute for Responsive Education (IRE)

605 Commonwealth Ave. Boston, MA 02215. A nonprofit research and advocacy organization working to make schools more responsive to citizen and parent involvement. Working closely with school districts around the country, IRE provides technical assistance and consulting aimed at promoting parental choice within public school systems. Publishes a journal triannually, *New Schools, New Communities* (formerly *Equity and Choice*).

National Association of Multicultural Education

Donna Gollnick, NAME membership chair 2101-A North Rolfe St., Arlington, VA 22209 703-243-4525. An organization committed to promoting multicultural education. Publishes a quarterly journal, *Multicultural Education* and holds an annual conference.

National Coalition of Advocates for Students

100 Boylston St., Suite 737, Boston MA 02116-4610; 617-357-8507. A coalition of 22 child advocacy groups in 14 states that works to achieve equal access to a quality public education for most vulnerable students, particularly those who are poor, children of color, recently immigrated, or differently abled. Makes available many good resources on school reform efforts such as *The Good Common School: Making the Vision Work for All Children.* Maintains the Clearinghouse for Immigrant Education and the National Center for Immigrant Students.

National Coalition of Education Activists

P.O. Box 679 Rhinebeck, NY 12572; 914-876-4580. A national multiracial network of parents, community members, teachers, and union activists working for progressive school reform. Holds an annual conference in the summer and distributes a quarterly newsletter, Action for Better Schools.

National Committee for Citizens in Education

900 2nd St. N.E. , Suite 8, Washington, DC; 202-408-0447. An organization working to expand parent and community access to public schools and build support for public school reform.

Network of Educators on the Americas (NCEA)

P.O. Box 73038 Washington, DC 20056-3038; 202-806-7277. A national nonprofit organization that works with schools and communities to develop and promote teaching methods and resources for social and economic justice in the Americas. These projects reflect NCEA's goal of promoting peace, justice and human rights through critical, antiracist, multicultural education. Distributes a catalogue of K–12 resources for antiracist, multicultural education, *Teaching for Change*.

Philadelphia Public School Notebook

3721 Midvale Ave. Philadelphia, PA. 19129-1532; 215-951-0330. A quarterly newspaper that provides a voice for parents, students, classroom teachers, and various groups in the Philadelphia area working for quality and equality in schools. The newspaper is a project of the New Beginnings Program of Resources for Human Development.

Rethinking Schools

1001 E. Keefe Ave., Milwaukee, WI 53212-1710; 414-964-9646. An independent journal written by parents, teachers and educational activists committed to achieving equity and social justice in public schooling and published four times per year in a newspaper format. *Rethinking Schools* has one overriding concern: to help transform our schools so they can help provide a quality education for all children. This group has also published three magazine format special editions, *Rethinking Our Classrooms: Teaching for Equity and Social Justice, Rethinking Columbus, and False Choices: Why School Vouchers Threaten Our Children's Future.*

School Voices

115 W. 28th St., Suite 3R, New York, NY 10001; 212-643-8490. A quarterly newspaper for "pro-equality educators, parents, and students of all races," sponsored by New York's People About Changing Education (PACE), a multiracial network of educators and parents.

Appendix B

A DIRECTORY OF PUBLICATIONS AND ORGANIZATIONS FOCUSING ON SUPPORTING AND SHARING TEACHER RESEARCH

Action Research of Wisconsin Network (AROW)

Formerly the Madison Area Action Research Network. Coordinator, Cathy Caro-Bruce, Madison Metropolitan School District, 545 W. Dayton St. Madison WI 53703. Sponsors action research groups and provides technical assistance to people wanting to start new groups. Publishes and distributes action research studies and holds an annual conference in the spring.

Alaska Teacher Research Network

Box 58480, Fairbanks, AK 99711. Distributes teacher research studies, publishes a newsletter, and sponsors teacher research conferences.

Collaborative Action Research Network

Coordinator, Bridget Somekh, Scottish Council for Research in Education 15 St. John St., Edinburgh EH8 8JR U.K. An international network of action researchers and those who write about action research. Holds an annual conference each fall in the UK and publishes *The Journal of Educational Action Research*, which contains some reports of teacher research.

Harvard Educator's Forum-Writing Exchange

Claryce Evans, Harvard University Graduate School of Education, Room 211 Longfellow Hall Appian Way, Cambridge MA 02138. Sponsors teacher research groups and distributes teacher research studies. Publications list available.

The Learning Exchange

3132 Pennsylvania Ave. Kansas City, MO 64111; 816-754-4150. Sponsors an annual international collaborative action research symposium in the spring.

The Massachusetts Field Center for Teaching and Learning

University of Massachusetts–Boston, 100 Morrissey Blvd. Boston, MA 02125. A statewide network focusing on teacher development and school improvement that publishes Teaching Voices. This newsletter contains reports of teacher research projects that are funded by the center. A complete listing of the studies is available in the publication Teacher-Researcher Program.

Teacher Research: The Journal of Classroom Inquiry

A journal published twice per year that includes teachers' reports of research from their own classrooms and articles about classroom inquiry. Editors: Ruth Hubbard *Teacher Research* Journal, Campus Box 14 Lewis and Clark College, Portland , OR 97219 and Brenda Power *Teacher Research Journal*, 5766 Shibles Hall, University of Maine, ORONO, ME 04469-5766.

Teaching and Change

A journal published four times annually. Provides an open forum for reporting the experiences of classroom teachers as they learn how schools must change to make good practice possible. Devoted to helping teachers as they work to strengthen their learning communities. Karen Zauber, Editor *Teaching and Change*, NEA-National Center for Innovation. 1201 16th St, NW, Washington, DC 20036.

REFERENCES

Apple, M. (1993). *Teachers and texts: A political economy of class and gender relations in education*. New York: Routledge.

Berliner, D. (1987). Knowledge is power. In D. Berliner & B. Rosenshine (Eds.), *Talks to teachers* (pp. 3–33). Toronto: Random House.

Beyer, L. (1988). *Knowing and acting: Inquiry, ideology, and educational studies*. London: Falmer Press.

Bielenberg, J. (1995). *Conceptions of science education*. Unpublished doctoral dissertation, University of Colorado at Boulder, School of Education, Boulder.

Britzman, D. (1991). *Practice makes practice: A critical study of learning to teach*. Albany, NY: SUNY Press.

Bullough, R., Knowles, J. G., & Crow, N. (1992). *Emerging as a teacher*. London: Routledge.

Calderhead, J. (1989). Reflective teaching and teacher education. *Teaching and Teacher Education, 5*(1), 43–51.

Carpenter, T., & Fennema, E. (1992). Cognitively guided instruction: Building on the knowledge of students and teachers. In W. Secada (Ed.), Curriculum reform: The case of mathematics in the U.S. [Special Issue]. *Instructional Journal of Educational Research*, 457–470.

Chamot, A., & O'Malley, J. M. (1994). *The CALLA Handbook*. Reading, MA: Addison-Wesley.

Clandinin, J., Davies, A., Hogan, P., & Kennard, B. (Eds.). (1993). *Learning to teach: Teaching to learn*. New York: Teacher's College Press.

Connelly, M., & Clandinin, J. (1988). *Teachers as curriculum planners: Narratives of experience*. New York: Teacher's College Press.

Cruickshank, D. (1987). *Reflective teaching*. Reston, VA: Association of Teacher Educators.

Cuban, L. (1984) *How teachers taught: Constancy and change in America's classrooms*. New York: Longman.

Darling-Hammond, L., & Berry, B. (1988). *The evolution of teacher policy*. Washington DC: Rand.

Darling-Hammond, L. (Ed.). (1994). *Professional development schools: Schools for developing a profession*. New York: Teacher's College Press.

Day, C. (1993). Reflection: A necessary but not sufficient condition for professional development. *British Educational Research Journal, 19*(1), 83–93.

Delpit, L. (1986). Skills and other dilemmas of a progressive black educator. *Harvard Educational Review*, *56*(4), .

Dewey, J. (1965). The relation of theory to practice in education. In M. Borrowman (Ed.), *Teacher education in America: A documentary history*. New York: Teacher's College Press. (Original work published 1904)

Dewey, J. (1933). *How we think*. Chicago: Henry Regnery.

Dewey, J. (1938). *Experience and education*. New York: Collier Books.

Duckworth, E. (1987). *The having of wonderful ideas*. New York: Teacher's College Press.

Elbaz, F. (1983). *Teacher thinking: A study of practical knowledge*. London: Croom Helm.

Elliot, J. (1991). *Action research for educational change*. Buckingham, UK: Open University Press.

Feiman-Nemser, S. (1990). Teacher preparation: Structural and conceptual alternatives. In W. R. Houston (Ed.), *Handbook of research on teacher education* (pp. 212–233). New York: Macmillan.

Fennema, E., Carpenter, T., & Franke, M. (in press). In M. L. Watt (Ed.), *Action research and the reform of mathematics & science education*. New York: Teacher's College Press.

Fenstermacher, G. (1980). On learning to teach effectively from research on teacher effectiveness. In C. Denham & A. Lieberman (Eds.), *Time to learn* (pp. 127–138). Washington, DC: U.S. Department of Education.

Freedman, S., Jackson, J., & Boles, K. (1983). Teaching: An imperiled profession. In L. Shulman & G. Sykes (Eds.), *Handbook of teaching and policy* (pp. 261–299). New York: Longman.

Gentile, J. R. (1988). *Instructional improvement: Summary and analysis of Madeline Hunter's essential elements of instruction and supervision*. Oxford, OH: National Staff Development Council.

Greene, M. (1986). Reflection and passion in teaching. *Journal of Curriculum and Supervision*, *2*(1), 68–81.

Griffiths, M., & Tann, S. (1992). Using reflective practice to link personal and public theories. *Journal of Education for Teaching*, *18*(1), 69–84.

Grossman, P. (1990). *The making of a teacher: Teacher knowledge and teacher education*. New York: Teacher's College Press.

Gutmann, A. (1987) *Democratic education*. Princeton, NJ: Princeton University Press.

Handal, G., & Lauvas, P. (1987). *Promoting reflective teaching*. Milton Keynes, UK: Open University Press.

Heath, S. B. (1983). *Ways with words* New York: Cambridge University Press.

Johnson, D., & Johnson, R. (1994). *Learning together and alone: cooperative, competitive and individualistic learning* (4th ed.). Needham Heights, MA: Allyn & Bacon.

Kemmis, S. (1985). Action research and the politics of reflection. In D. Boud, R. Keogh, & D. Walker (Eds.), *Reflection: Turning experience into learning* (pp. 139–164). London: Croom Helm.

Lakoff, G., & Johnson, M. (1980). *Metaphors we live by*. Chicago: University of Chicago Press.

Lieberman, A., & Miller, L. (1991). *Staff development for the 1990's: New demands, new realities, new perspectives* (2nd ed.). New York: Teacher's College Press.

Lightfoot, S. L. (1978). *Worlds apart*. New York: Basic Books.

Liston, D. P., & Zeichner, K. M. (1991). *Teacher education and the social conditions of schooling*. New York: Routledge.

Lytle, S., & Cochran-Smith, M. (1990). Learning from teacher research: A working typology. *Teachers College Record*, *92*(1), 83–103.

Marshall, H. (1990). Metaphor as an instructional tool in encouraging student teacher reflection. *Theory into Practice, 29*(2), 128–132.

McDiarmid, G. W. (1992). *The arts and sciences as preparation for teaching.* East Lansing, MI: National Center for Research on Teacher Learning.

Meloth, M., & Derring, P. (1991). Task talk and task awareness under different cooperative learning conditions. *American Educational Research Journal, 31*(1), 138–165.

Meloth, M., & Deering, P. (1992). Effects of two cooperative conditions on peer group discussions, reading comprehension and metacognition. *Contemporary Educational Psychology, 17,* 175–193.

Munby, H., & Russell, T. (1990). Metaphor in the study of teachers' professional knowledge. *Theory into Practice, 29*(2), 116–121.

Osterman, K., & Kottkamp, R. (1993). *Reflective practice for educators.* Newbury Park, CA: Corwin Press.

Paris, C. (1993). *Teacher agency and curriculum making in classrooms.* New York: Teacher's College Press.

Perrone, V. (1989). *Working papers: Reflections on teachers, schools and community.* New York: Teacher's College Press.

Peterson, R. (1993). Creating a school that honors the traditions of a culturally diverse student body: La Escuela Fratney. In G.A. Smith (Ed.), *Public schools that work* (pp. 45–67). New York: Routledge.

Pollard, A., & Tann, S. (1994). *Reflective teaching in the primary school* (2nd ed.). London: Cassell.

Popkewitz, T. (1991). *A political sociology of educational reform.* New York: Teacher's College Press.

Rosenholtz, S. J. (1989). *Teachers' workplace: The social organization of schools.* New York: Longman.

Ross, D., & Kyle, D. (1987). Helping preservice teachers learn to use teacher effectiveness research. *Journal of Teacher Education, 38,* 40–44.

Ruddick, J., & Hopkins, D. (1985). *Research as the basis for teaching.* London: Heinemann Books.

Ruenz, D. (1994, September). A lesson in tolerance. *Teacher,* pp. 25–29.

Sarason, S. (1971). *The culture of the school and the problem of change.* Boston: Allyn & Bacon.

Scheffler, I. (1968). University scholarship and the education of teachers. *Teachers College Record, 70*(1), 1–12.

Schon, D. (1983). *The reflective practitioner.* New York: Basic Books.

Schon, D. (1987). *Educating the reflective practitioner.* San Francisco: Jossey-Bass.

Schwab, J. (1971). The practical: Arts of eclectic. *School Review, 79,* 493–543.

Shulman, L. (1986). Those who understand: Knowledge growth in teaching. *Educational Researcher, 15*(2), 4–14.

Smith, B. O., Peterson, D., & Micceri, T. (1987). Evaluation and professional improvement aspects of the Florida performance measurement system. *Educational Leadership, 44*(7), 16–19.

Solomon, J. (1987). New thoughts on teacher education. *Oxford Review of Education, 13*(3), 267–74.

Tabachnick, B. R., & Zeichner, K. M. (1991). *Issues and practices in inquiry-oriented teacher education.* London: Falmer Press.

Thomas, L. (1974). *The lives of a cell.* New York: Bantam.

Tremmel, R. (1993). Zen and the art of reflective practice. *Harvard Educational Review, 63*(4), 434–458.

Valli, L. (1990). *The question of quality and content in reflective teaching*. Paper presented at the annual meeting of the American Educational Research Association, Boston, MA.

Valli, L.(1993). Reflective teacher education programs: An analysis of case studies. In J. Calderhead (Ed.), *Conceptualizing reflection in teacher development* (pp. 11–22). Albany, NY: SUNY Press.

Wilson, S., Shulman, L., & Richert, A. (1987). 150 different ways of knowing: Representations of knowledge in teaching. In J. Calderhead (Ed.), *Exploring teachers' thinking* (pp. 104–124). London: Cassell.

Wise, A. (1979). *Legislated learning*. Berkeley: University of California Press.

Wood, P. (1988). Action research: A field perspective. *Journal of Education for Teaching 14*(2), 135–150.

Zumwalt, K. (1982). Research on teaching: Policy implications for teacher education. In A. Lieberman & M. McLaughlin (Eds.), *Policy making in education* (pp. 215–248). Chicago: University of Chicago Press.

INDEX